SWIM

like you run

Triathlon Books by Bill Hammons

The Indoor Triathlete

Swim

Bill Hammons

SWIM

like you run

Bill Hammons

Hafta Books
Atlanta MMXI

ISBN 978-0-9831263-1-7

Written by Bill Hammons

Designed by Archie Delapaz
www.turrtlebeachstudios.com

Pictures by Atwell Photography
www.atwellphotography.com

Printed in the United States of America

Dedicated to my teachers, coaches, students and athletes.

Contents

Introduction

If you could swim as fast as you walk, say a fifteen minute mile or faster, you could be a world champion. The record for a one mile swim is in the range of of fourteen and a half minutes. While it might be unrealistic to swim as fast you walk, some people do swim as easily as they walk.

To swim like you run, you are going to learn, to do in the water, all of those activities that you take for granted while running: seeing, breathing, and arms leading the body.

Your inner ear and eyes help you stay balanced while you run. Many people have not learned, nor are aware, of the importance of training their eyes and ears for swimming.

Your core strength, which includes your abdominal and back muscles, support you while you run. Many people have not learned to keep their core engaged while swimming.

Your breathing, your inhales and exhales, is not restricted while running. Many people need to learn to exhale underwater in order to maximize the time for inhaling above water when swimming.

Your legs are very purposeful when running. Many people have swim kicks that are not purposeful. They have compensating kicks that are sporadic, erratic and often too wide.

Your arms lead your body and set the tone for your body and legs when running. Some people swim with arms completely out of sync with their legs and body.

Your flexibility, or lack of it, effects your run and you adjust for it. It's the same with swimming. You can adjust your swimming, like you do running ,for your lack of flexibility.

Your legs and arms bend when you run. Your stride adjusts for the conditions when you run. You realize that faster running means breathing faster and harder. You slow your run down to be comfortable. These conditions also apply to swimming as they do to running.

Many people already feel like they are running or sprinting as fast as they can from one end of the pool to the other while swimming. There is a big difference between speeding up your stroke for efficiency versus speeding up your stroke because you are afraid of sinking and drowning.

When I take my stroke from a walking pace to running, I change from a two stroke pattern to a three stroke pattern. The tempo increases from forty strokes a minutes at my walking pace to sixty strokes a minute at my running pace in the water.

At a running swimming tempo, I don't want to extend the time between inhales so I increase the tempo to get to the next inhale sooner. There can be a different economy to running that you don't find with walking or skating. There are different energy expenditures in swimming when going from a running tempo to a walking tempo or to skating tempo while swimming.

Some swimmers have a gliding motion, much like a skater. When swimming with gliding motions, you can create a feeling similar to the feeling skaters have while moving over ice. You bear your weight longer on one side until you shift your weight to the other side. After you shift your weight to the other side, your skate blade shifts from a straight ahead gliding position to a sideways position to hold or catch the ice because you want to some traction on a very slippery surface. So, at the propulsive moment in skating you have a weight shift with a leg moving forward and a leg seemingly moving backwards (when in effect, the backward leg is trying not to go backwards because it wants to hold the ice so you don't fall while propelling yourself forward).

You probably have noticed that most beginning skaters and swimmers act alike. Beginning skaters and swimmers make more motions than they would need to to keep from falling or sinking while not going very far on the ice or in the water.

However, skaters seem to realize, faster than swimmers, not to mistake a high level of activity with progress. Mistakenly, some people think that they will get to be better swimmers by continuing to stroke and kick faster and harder. Maybe due to falling on the hard surface of the ice, skaters debunk the faster and harder method of learning to skate earlier than swimmers do in the water.

For whatever reason, some swimmers stick with faster and harder activity over slower and easier. Maybe it is due to seeing Olympic swim events that are basically sprints in the water. Or maybe it is watching children swim twenty-five, fifty and one hundred yard events that perpetuates the faster and harder approach to swimming that influences fewer people to learn to swim with a glide and lower activity level.

Your size does have an effect on your ability to glide on ice or in the water. The bigger person can glide farther on the ice and in the water. The smaller swimmer or skater weighing one hundred pounds takes two movements to the two hundred pound swimmer or skater of equal ability, because momentum equals mass times velocity. Yet, sometimes it is easier for the smaller person to take two movements than it is for the bigger person to take two movements. Your size is to your advantage when you can coordinate your movements.

When learning to swim you would benefit from approaching swimming like skating, too. If you weigh under one hundred and fifty pounds, then you will probably want to kick and stroke more often like a small skater. If you weigh over one hundred and fifty pounds, then you can kick and stroke less, like a large skater. Short swimming distances are like sprints and both large and small people can sprint (though the smaller swimmer tends to get up to speed faster and then they try to maintain that advantage). Long swimming distances can favor heavy swimmers. Longer distances favor the larger swimmer's glide in between strokes without kicking.

It's not solely height or length or arm length that are the dominant advantages in swimming and skating, it is also mass or weight that makes the difference. While height and long arms help and correlate to a person's weight, it is difficult for a skinny, tall person to out swim a heavier, tall person of equal ability. So, while the tall swimmer or skater often has a harder time learning to control their longer levers, their arms and legs, the shorter swimmer or skater often has an easier time learning to control their short levers, their arms and legs. Learning to skate or swim when you are young is often better because it is easier to teach the gross motor skills when the levers, arms and legs, are still small.

Your future is about to change, if you choose to change. You may have been a poor swimmer, yet you may become the best swimmer, the most knowledgeable swimmer, from your school twenty to forty years later if you adopt, borrow and learn from the information in this book.

Let's review the information that many people have had swimming. For most, swimming began while standing or sitting in the water. You could see the horizon and you were either on the firm bottom of the pool or a softer, smooshy, natural surface. You still had a visual and physical, spatial horizon and orientation.

You wondered how people left their feet and swam. Anytime you weren't in contact with the bottom, your inner ear experienced a loss of equilibrium and your vision was restricted underwater.

You were told to hold your breath underwater to avoid inhaling water. You played games to see how long you could hold your breath. Bobbing up for air and then bobbing down was probably the next activity. Bobbing reinforced spatial orientation and breath holding skills. You began to learn how to be underwater for brief periods with fewer visual skills and developed some tactile skills. Like a pilot not wanting to lose the horizon for long, you wanted to get back to the surface.

When you learned to tread water, you were probably pleased that you had your visual horizon back. Swimming, for you, might be about keeping your head above water so you do not have to lose track of the surface or hold your breath. And while treading water took substantial effort, it was worth being able to breathe and see where you were.

So you progressed in swimming by treading water less vertically to swimming more diagonally in order to keep your head out of the water so as not to lose your horizon and run out of air. It took a lot of effort to swim this way, yet swimming is exercise and exercise is supposed to be hard and frustrating according to some people. So you thought, that eventually, enough exercise could allow you to swim for miles with your head out of the water, if you just kept it up. You thought that you just needed to work harder to swim better.

Kicking helped keep your head out of the water when your arms couldn't, and kicking hard in the water is more exercise. Perhaps you thought, "Wow this swimming is really great (meaning hard) exercise".

And your paddling or stroking, was real exercise too. You had to keep your arms moving to keep your head out of the water and move somewhere. Swimming could be an exhausting, full body workout. It is rather interesting that there are some adult swimmers who don't want better swim technique because they like how hard swimming is for them. They honestly say that they want the effort or the exercise more than they want to learn better technique or increase performance.

On the other hand, you might be one of those swimmers who progressed and began putting your head underwater. You either brought your head straight forward and up for air or to the side for air. You probably brought your head up though because your inner ear probably had fewer problems with that maneuver than the rolling to the side. You probably did not realize how much your inner ear was determining your ability to swim.

Under the water's surface, you were probably focusing on what some people call paddling, the catch and pull, or I refer to it as the row. You might think of it as your hand pushing backwards and downwards so you can go forward and upward. And,you may have thought the way to go faster swimming is to paddle or row faster and with more effort.

You still kicked hard because kicking helped get your head out of the water. Like most people, you wanted oxygen and your horizon so you could get to your destination.

You might have thought that, one of these days, you would be in great shape because swimming requires so much effort.

If you hung in there long enough, you may have learned how to do an underwater flip turn. Talk about a piloting challenge, an underwater flip turn is the loop de loop of the swim world. You really are in control of your inner ear if you know which way is up while flipping underwater.

So your history of swimming probably involved effort, breath holding, paddling and little awareness of how your inner ear and eyes influenced your swimming.

With this program, I want you to modify or vary my techniques to match your characteristics. First of all, there is no one size fits all swim technique. The way Olympic gold medalist Michael Phelps swam would not fit how Olympic gold medalist Janet Evans swam. You will learn my principles of swimming and then apply the principles to you. You could call your stroke, _____'s stroke. You will learn about approaches that you can use while swimming based on your characteristics and then adapt and apply the ideas.

While my swimmers have a definite "look" (due to the thumbs up technique to keep your shoulders healthy and improve performance) each one of my swimmers swims differently because they modify the techniques for a custom fit. For example, if you weigh less, you are likely to need more strokes per lap. Or, if your foot and ankle are not very flexible, you will bend your knee more while kicking. Because physical and mental characteristics come in multiples, you will have a custom swim stroke if you apply the principles to you.

Chapter One – Freestyle spatial orientation.

Pilot your swim.

You may not realize how you are always "piloting". Like a pilot you want a visual or tactile horizon for your inner ear or you get disoriented, maybe even to the point of being dizzy or seasick. While the inability to breathe sufficiently is the most common complaint, especially by beginners, the real problem may begin with a loss of equilibrium and a person being anxious about not seeing where the next breath of air is.

While swimming, your "horizon" is the surface of the water. It helps you to see the surface as much as you need. Some people begin by not putting their head under the water so they can always see their horizon. Some people can barely stand putting their head underwater for very brief periods. Some people go to the other extreme though and try to swim the length of the pool without breathing so they don't lose sight of the bottom of the pool for visual orientation. Whereas, if they rolled up for air, that would disorient them.

Learn how to be a good "pilot" in the water if you want to swim well. Like a pilot, you will need to learn how to use fewer and fewer visual clues and more tactile skills. An example of a reduced visual cue would be seeing no farther your arm in front of you in dark and murky water. An example of a tactile clue would be feeling the surface of the water with your hand or water pressure on your hand. You can learn to swim with fewer visual and tactile skills like pilots do.

The dominant swimming pattern.

The dominant swimming pattern is breathing to one side. Breathing to one's "best" side allows a person to look and breathe more easily and with greater swimming speed.

Beginners often think that it is better to go four, six or eight strokes before taking a breath. Incorrectly, they think that breathing less often is an improvement in fitness. Yet, we seldom apply that reasoning to other aerobic sports that benefit from breathing more often like running or cycling. Breathing less often while swimming is actually a sign that a person has trouble rolling up for air.

Breathing is the number one problem for many swimmers It appears that the problem could be in the hips because the hips tend to sink when going for air. Perhaps the hips were not as strong on one side as the other. Strong core muscles and core awareness helps, yet more is needed.

Moving elsewhere to help breathing, a thumbs up hand position helps the roll for air by being in agreement with your shoulder and body. The lack of flexibility in one's shoulder with a thumbs down or flat hand creates trouble while rolling for air because it cuts short your inhale when the leading hand and arm sinks in the water prematurely to prevent shoulder pain and injury.

Further moving around the body, it could that the dominant eye and inner ear and neck flexibility determine your "best" side to roll for air. Swimmers with one eye, roll up on the side where they can see the surface. We can train ourselves to breath to both sides by training the eye and inner ear on both sides.

Maintain your balance by seeing a horizon.

You can maintain your equilibrium or balance by constantly keeping your head out of the water. I don't recommend this approach though because it requires more energy and can be slow. Some swim strokes do this better than others. Sidestroke and backstroke are the two strokes where you can keep your head out of the water 100% of the time efficiently. The breaststroke is much less efficient when you keep your head out of the water on the other hand. You can also keep your head out of the water with freestyle, although it takes a great deal of effort and looks less like freestyle. Whereas, the butterfly stroke requires that you put your head underwater.

Lifeguards often keep their heads out of water while swimming. Yet, the purpose for doing so is to keep sight of the person that they are swimming towards. A lifeguard does not want to visually lose contact with someone in trouble. Therefore, lifeguards give up some speed for safety.

To swim efficiently, you want to level off in the water like a pilot levels off in the air. Leveling off in the water will require that you put your head underwater where your visual orientation is lessened or lost. Underwater, you will be on autopilot, or flying by "instruments", or the way it feels.

Close to the surface, you can still feel when a hand, arm or leg is above or below water. In this way, you know where the surface or horizon is, too. In shallow water, touching bottom can give you a feel for horizontal.

Maintain your balance by seeing a temporary horizon.

Many people swim with their head underwater as long as they can because it's easier than coming up for air off balance. Most people feel off balance, especially when rolling to the side for air, because their inner ear, hand and arm, and core muscles are not trained. Yet, you can train your inner ear, hand and arm and core. And, you will learn faster if you roll and breathe more often. Rolling for air less often does not give you the frequency of practice that you will need to change your muscle memory. In this program, breathing every other stroke, or two strokes, will have you practicing a balanced roll fifty percent of the time more than breathing every three strokes. Additionally, you will be training your inner ear, eyes, hands, arms and core on one side at a time in order to learn each side well.

One of the reasons that some swimmers take longer breaths or looks than others, is that they want more visual orientation when swimming. A glance of the surface, may not be enough for their inner ear to maintain an horizon. In addition to your need for sufficient air, is the need not to feel dizzy or lost while swimming.

Looking around more often and for short intervals is good piloting. We look around us a great deal when we are driving a car or piloting an aircraft. We are taught and teach ourselves not to fixate on something for long periods or we lose track of where we when moving. I tell my swimmers to practice taking more frequent and shorter looks when rolling for air. It seems to be easier for someone to adopt the suggestion to look quickly compared to the suggestion to inhale more quickly. Some people might be anxious if they were told to breathe more quickly. Yet, looking quickly also has them inhaling more quickly with less anxiety.

19

Develop your ability to look left and right more easily on land and in the water. You can do balance and neck exercises on land to develop your ability to look more easily, more often in the water.

Visually it helps your equilibrium when your arms are in front of you when swimming. It also give you physical confidence. If you are always paddling when you swim, you probably won't see or feel your arms in front of you for long. If you adapt my swimming techniques, you will have a hand and arm leading you through the water.

Here are some ideas to give you a flavor of these techniques. A feeling that I like to have while swimming is when my arm is out of the water and my fingers are "running" on the water's surface. Touching the water's surface with your fingertips gives you great tactile feedback. You know just where the surface is. Increasing the speed of your fingers over the water when taking a stroke, increases your speed easily. What your hand and arm does above the water provides important feedback to your inner ear when you maintain some contact with the surface. With my swim techniques, fingers touching the water's surface also sets up a strong "throw" right to the place underwater where you to begin your catch and pull or "row".

Paying attention to your hands and arms above the water is just as important as paying attention to your hands and arms below the water. A good "throw" and a good "row", that work together, create a beautiful stroke that is half the effort of making one arm do all the work.

Children wobble when learning to walk. Children even wobble when learning to stand until they engage their core muscles, too. And when we wobble, at any age, it's as much about our inner ear that controls our balance as our feet.

We learn muscle memory on land that satisfies the inner ear requirement for spatial orientation. In the water, you can swim like you walk. You can learn muscle memories and positions that are more stable than others and that satisfy your inner ear.

Wide, outspread arms are more stable (and powerful) then arms closer to the body. Swimming with your arms crossed just in front of your head is like walking a tight rope. Learn to swim with arms wide, in front of your shoulders, for more stability and power.

Rhythm also helps satisfy the inner ear. An erratic walking or swimming style keeps the inner ear guessing what is coming next. You will learn how to develop a rhythm and smooth out your stroke, especially when rolling for a breath of air. And breathing consistently and predictably, will also keep you from hurrying those strokes you take before you breathe.

Looking every other stroke or the two stroke pattern.

Looking and breathing every other stroke has several big advantages. As a pilot, you are satisfying your need for spatial orientation. Whether that is seeing the water's surface, shore, boat or another swimmer, spatial orientation helps you swim with more confidence.

Breathing every other stroke maximizes your aerobic growth. Not breathing promotes anaerobic gains rather than aerobic gains which are more valuable. You do experience limited gains by not breathing; but, you do reach a physiological limit, at a higher cost, anaerobically. Breathing every other stroke seems more like walking or skating to me.

Breathing every third stroke could be closer to the rate that you breathe on land while running. While running it is typical to take about ninety steps in a minute. Inhaling every fourth step means about twenty-two breaths a minute. If you take sixty strokes to go fifty yards in one minute, then you would be breathing twenty times when breathing every third stroke. Or, if your took forty strokes breathing every other or every two strokes, you would still be breathing twenty times a minute. Breathing at the same rate that you breathe on land and in the water is physiological wisdom.

Once you resolve your eye and inner ear challenge and don't lose your balance while rolling for air, breathing every other stroke can be faster over distance. Breathing often does not have to slow you down. Being disoriented when rolling for a breath does slow you down. Being out of breath, from not breathing often enough, also slows you down.

Train your dominant side first to breath every other stroke. Repetition helps you get better, faster. Putting off two stroke breathing only hinders progress. For example if you go four strokes before breathing, you are practicing your roll for air 100% less often than every other stroke. Also you are four stokes rather than just two strokes past your last memory of rolling for air. I would like you to have to the visual, inner ear and tactile memory of the roll to air more frequently, so you can alter what is not working and learn what is working for you.

Your non-dominant side can learn the roll for air too. In fact, some have so many habits to break on the dominant side that they may actually improve faster on their non-dominant side.

I have a kicking drill for you later in this book that goes well with the two stroke pattern. It will help you to improve your roll to air on one side and then the other side. Even with this drill though, you will need to pay attention and concentrate on keeping your arm in front of you before, during and after you roll up for air while swimming for spatial orientation.

Learn to see and breathe to both sides for many reasons. During a triathlon, your vision might be hindered by the sun or something else. If you breathe only to one side, you create muscle and flexibility imbalances that can cause you problems later. You may also find that you swim straighter on your slower or weaker side. Swimming straighter may be faster in the open water than using your dominant side that powers you off course faster. And, if you determine that overpowering your stroke on your dominant side takes you off course, then you will probably adjust your dominant side, too.

Looking every third stroke of the three stroke pattern.

"Why did the swimmer take three strokes? Answer: To get to the other side.", is a weak joke. Yet, it is true. As a swimmer if you can only look or breathe to one side, you are limiting what you can see. A good pilot or driver looks both ways.

It's important to be able to change the side that you are looking towards. There are times when the sun will blind you, the waves will annoy you, and another swimmer will be in your way. When those situations exist, it's time to take three strokes to see if the other side is better. Neither side maybe that great, yet you want to feel like you have an option to look and breathe to the side that's best for you at that time.

It's more challenging to look or breathe every third stroke because both inner ears and both eyes need to be trained to two horizons, one to the left and one to the right. It is easier to know visually and tactically that the horizon is on one side. It's harder to conceptualize an horizon left and right, because they can be physically different. One side may be shore and one side may be ocean. And when you are then looking underwater in between those two options, it could be challenging to take it all in and get used to the changes while swimming.

Breathing can also be a bigger challenge to both sides. You may lack neck or shoulder flexibility and the roll to one for air may be much harder or easier on that side. You will also be breathing fifty percent less often, if you try to maintain the same stroke distance as the two stroke pattern.

Work with your neck and shoulder flexibility. Like Mark Twain said, walk your habits down the stairs instead of throwing them out the upstairs window to get rid of them. In other words, you are going to hurt yourself if you expect and try to make years of neck or shoulder strain go away in a day, week or month. Start to improve your flexibility today. Expect the change in flexibility to take a year. Your stroke in the three stroke pattern is different than your stroke in the two stroke pattern. Breathing fifty percent less is really not a desirable option for many distance swimmers. Something has to give. The easiest place to manage the give and take is to allow the stroke length to be fifty percent shorter over the three strokes. Or, in other words, the three strokes are going to be fifty percent faster than the two strokes.

Your three stroke pattern is going to feel faster, like running, because you want to get to your next breath faster. The two stroke pattern is going to feel like taking big strides on land or on ice skates. The three stoke patten is going to feel like taking shorter strides.

You could also want a three stroke pattern when swimming against a current for example. Like running, there are times when it is better to take three shorter, quicker steps rather than two big ones. The three stroke pattern can be like a smaller gear on a bike compared to a bigger gear, when it's beneficial to take three quicker strokes rather than two slower strokes.

The three stroke pattern is not better nor worse than a two stroke pattern. Both stroke patterns have important uses. Develop both patterns and think of them as two tools to help you swim better.

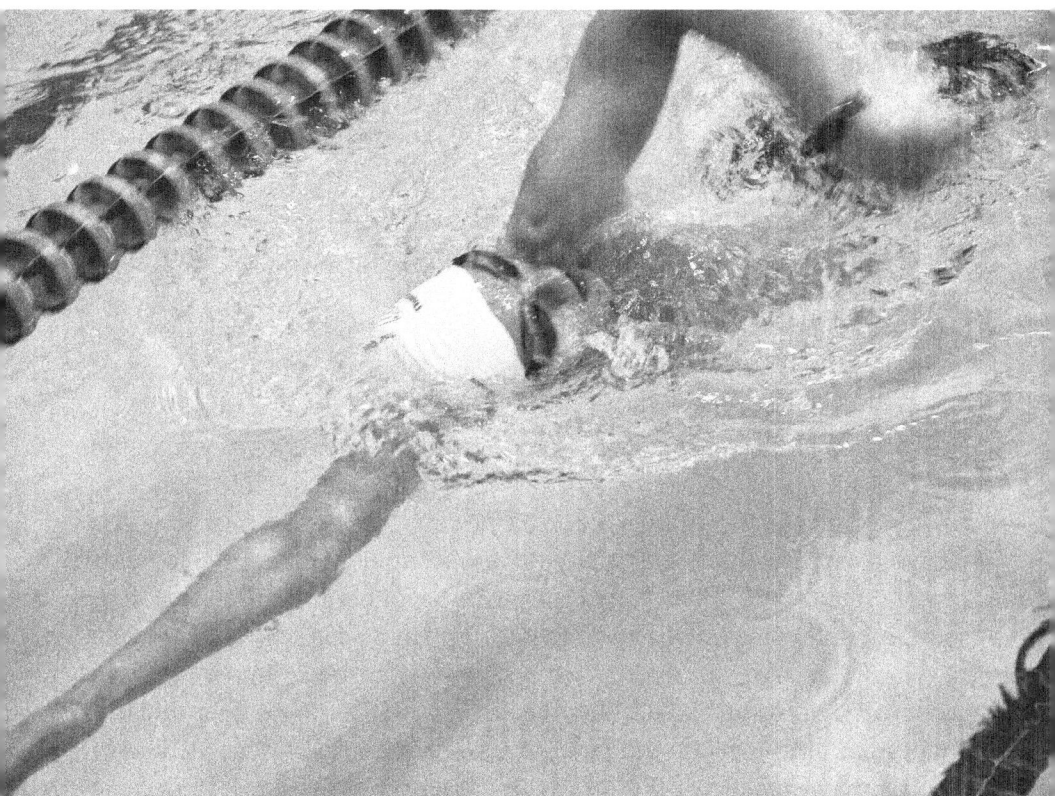

Chapter Two – Freestyle breathing.

Completely aerobic swimming.

I recommend that you keep your swimming and triathlon training aerobic. You can win without going into oxygen debt, without creating lactic acid and without upsetting your body's chemistry. In fact, more often than not, going into deep oxygen debt during a race is a sign that you are about to fall off the pace and lose contact.

What is winning? For some, it is nothing less than first place. You win most distance races because your aerobic threshold is higher than the other person. In my prime, I was running at a 5:30 mile pace for close to two hours. I was running aerobically long after others were not, even though they were better anaerobically trained than I was.

For many, winning is doing well given their situation. Winning could be finishing. Winning could be health without much, if any racing. My definition of winning is broad and it goes from first place to showing up for the workout and being alive, as those over sixty years old remark.

Keeping your workout solely aerobic is hard to do. You may go anaerobic as much as five to ten percent of the time during your workout without meaning to do so. During a timed swim, you could be swimming at what you think is your aerobic limit only to discover, a few laps later, that you are swimming too fast and you are out of breath, filling up with lactic acid and having to slow down. You could also overextend a fast technical drill and go into oxygen debt. In your own efforts to improve, you will still go into oxygen debt. Anaerobically, we have about fifteen minutes of total anaerobic training in us. People who are training anaerobically, really can only sustain an anaerobic pace for fifteen minutes before they have to drop back to an aerobic pace to recover. They may be swimming for an hour, yet forty-five minutes of that hour is aerobic swimming mixed in with the anaerobic. In other words, even anaerobic swimmers are doing more aerobic swimming than they might realize.

This is an important point. If you are aerobic at your swim pace and the other swimmer can not keep up, then you are not going to lose. On the other hand, if you have to swim anaerobically to keep up with them, then the finish line better not be far away because no one can sustain an anaerobic swimming pace for long distances. From your own experience of doing laps in the pool, you quickly know whether the person in the next lane is passing you aerobically or anaerobically. If they have to stop at the end of the pool to breathe, while you continue to swim lap after lap, they were swimming anaerobically.

We improve at the cellular level. It's healthier to improve aerobically at the cellular level. The byproducts of anaerobic activity are called "waste" because your body will have to get rid of the byproducts of anaerobic production to return to health. Aerobic swimming is the healthiest way to train. As a distance swimmer, I want you to win because you have a high aerobic threshold and your technique is good.

Good technique and aerobic swimming go better together, too. If you are swimming aerobically, you can actually think clearly about your technique. On the other hand, if you are swimming anaerobically, your thoughts could be split between technique and when is that interval going to be over so you can catch your breath. Faster anaerobic swimming can also mask technical errors, like a lack of balance, if you slowed the movement down. Keep your swimming aerobic so you can improve your technique. Perhaps it's human nature, to think incorrectly, that the way to swim "right" will just come one of these days at one of those moments. We are hopeful, like a child with a drum set, that if we play fast and hard, one of these days, it will be "right". It is so much easier on everyone else in the house if we can convince the child to slow down and take some lessons to learn what "right" is before they try to do "right" fast (and loud).

Slow swimming can be more of technical challenge than fast swimming. Many people try to hide or make up for bad technique with effort. It's similar to hitting the golf ball hard or fast rather than well. Yes, sometimes that will work for a person with poor technique, yet it doesn't consistently work for them because their technique is still sporadic and erratic. A good musician tries to keep the music sounding good whether playing fast or slow. If the music falls apart when playing slowly, that reveals as much or more than technique falling apart at a higher speed.

Aerobic swimming gives you more time to practice technique while improving aerobically. You can achieve multiple goals while doing one activity. While you are raising your aerobic swimming pace, you can be improving your technique too. While you are increasing the time and distance that you can swim, you are also increasing the time and distance that you can practice your technique. Imagine a thirty minute or more swim where your feet never touch the bottom of the pool and you work on nearly every aspect of your swim stoke. You go from warmup, to doing swimming drills, to swimming without putting your feet on the bottom of the pool for a half hour or more. Consider a ten minute warm up or warm down swim where you go further without straining. It happens because your technique and aerobic threshold improved.

Besides aerobic gains propelling your improvement, technical gains propel your improvement. Good golfers can probably play eighteen holes to my nine, in the same amount of time, because their technique is so much better than mine. And the good golfers did not get better than me by playing faster, going harder or holding their breath. Good golfers got there at the cellular lever, aerobically, with good technique.

Swimming is the golf of the triathlon. A triathlon would not be much different if they asked a bunch of people to start out by playing nine or eighteen holes and then hop on a bike and do a run to determine the winner. There could still be people out on the golf course while some are finishing the bike.

Breathing with long exhales and short inhales.

Think about your breathing pattern every time you go for a swim. If you spend over ninety percent of your time, breathing whenever you want on land, you probably have to think about when you are going to breathe when you first get in the water.

One of the keys to your success in the water is using your nose for your long exhale. A long exhale achieves two goals for you: it rids you of carbon dioxide and it can keep water out of your nose.

You can feel out of breath, even though you have been inhaling while you swim. Many beginners often hold their breath underwater and then try to inhale on top of their last inhale. Just inhaling is like gasping for breath, a condition that many people describe after they swim just twenty-five or fifty yards.

You must clear your lungs underwater as you take your strokes. If you have to choose between thinking about exhaling and thinking about your swim stroke, choose to think about your underwater exhale first. A long exhale is every bit as important as a long swim stroke. While a short exhale is better than none, a short exhale does mean that you are partially storing some carbon dioxide rather than releasing the used air. Overtime, partial exhales add up and you feel out of breath.

It's a good plan to begin every swim with a warm up. Your first ten minutes in the water is about seeing and getting your exhale working for you. With every stroke, think exhale, exhale and exhale. Remember that for ninety plus percent of the day you were probably breathing unrestricted. Now you have to think about exhaling because your breathing is restricted by the water.

Fortunately, all it takes is a short inhale to fill the lungs with air. This is fortunate because rolling for air can be awkward and not as fast as heads down swimming. The fact that we can exhale for seconds underwater and then inhale in an instant plays right into our desire to spend more time with our head down swimming.

If you feel like you need to inhale more, then consider that you may really be missing the exhales between those inhales. While running, it does feel like you have to inhale more too. Yet, in reality, you need the exhales to get rid of the carbon dioxide first. It is the carbon dioxide in the blood that is making you feel breathless, so exhale it first to allow oxygen its place. While running or cycling practice exhaling too and see if you notice a performance benefit. Then be sure to exhale underwater, while swimming, to get the same benefit.

While you could wear a nose clip, exhaling from your nose will keep the water out of your nose. A benefit of exhaling from the nose and inhaling from the mouth is the division of labor. You train yourself that the air goes in your mouth quickly and out your nose more slowly. Some people find it difficult to exhale from their nose. Take time underwater to see your exhale bubble from your nose if this is the case. Sit or crouch in the water and notice the rate of exhale. A common progression is to go from breath holding, to exhaling in a burst or bursts, and finally to exhaling in a long stream of air.

You will be amazed at the volume of air that your lungs hold. Your lungs hold six liters of air and you exhale two to three liters with each breath. Seeing two to three liters of air, in bubble form, underwater gives you an appreciation for how much air you do hold with each breath. Because you hold a lot of air, get rid of the used air. The body defensively keeps a residual volume of a liter or more so your lungs don't collapse. So instead of exhaling just one to two liters at rest, an exhale of three to four liters will help increase your performance. You do have enough air in your lungs for a long exhale out your nose to keep your nose clear of water. Keep the exhale steady and you will also have enough remaining to blow a little air, like a whale or a porpoise, as you roll to the surface.

Your gains in swimming can come from two areas of improvement. Increasing your aerobic capacity will increase your endurance and speed. Increasing your technique will increase also your endurance and speed.

Distance swimmers, swimming for thirty minutes or more, are aerobic swimmers. For example, you can't run ten kilometers anaerobically. So, when training for a 10K run or longer, you do more long runs rather than interval runs. You can steadily improve your running and your swimming with aerobic training and never have to do intervals where you are breathless and upset your body's chemistry with lactic acid.

One of the problems with anaerobic training, is that you do reach the point where your technique falls apart. You go from the stroke that you are trying to develop to flailing in the water. Because swimming is the golf of the triathlon, hurrying your stroke to the point of failure is not going to help you get out the water faster. Imagine how a golfer's stroke would fall apart if the golfer had to play anaerobically. If a golf stroke did improve by playing golf anaerobically, they would be doing it.

Your training is going to be aerobic so your stroke does not fall apart and remains a highly efficient and technical stroke. You will be doing fast short, twenty-five yards or less, speed bursts to sharpen your stroke. Short, fast efforts stop before you go anaerobic. Yet, most of the time you will be swimming aerobically thinking about an aspect of your swim. A small portion of the time you will be doing some above race pace swimming in short segments to improve. Both the aerobic swimming and short, fast bursts will improve your technique and speed.

One concern with swimming anaerobic intervals is the same as basing your running or cycling on doing intervals on the track. The most common response to doing track intervals is a physical and mental burnout that leads to a lessening of the desire to train and results that flatten out and then decline. While intervals can help top competitors peak, they can also take the edge off them too. If you don't understand the limits of interval training, your desire could overcome your better judgment on how much to do.

Good results are more consistently achieved by improving your aerobic capacity and quality of your swim. As your times or distances improve, they will improve because what used to be an anaerobic speed for you is now an aerobic speed for you. Aerobically you can improve from running ten minute miles to running nine or eight minute miles or even five minute miles. Aerobically in the pool you can increase your speed while never doing long, hard intervals. You can swim like you walk, run or skate.

No matter how practiced you are at swimming, it's smart to think about your exhale at the beginning of every swim.

Occasionally, during a bike or a run when I am going fast, at the top edge of my aerobic capacity, I realize that I need to exhale more to "catch" my breath. During races, I also think about the exhale when beginning the bike or run. Working the exhale, also has had the effect of dropping my heart rate about five beats per minute.

Swimming demands even more focus than running or cycling. Your breathing is restricted. You are no longer moving through air but a liquid that is almost a hundred times thicker than air at the speed you want to go. You might as well be running in mud, and when you run in mud, it requires more breathing too.

To have your swim begin well, establish your sighting and breathing right away.

Chapter Three – Freestyle weight positioning

A boat or a barge is a very economical form of transit. One of the easiest, cheapest (and slowest) ways to ship people or goods is by water. A floating object in the water is easy to move. People can pull boats in the water that they could not budge on land. Some people, who can't swim, can float in the water like a barge. And, they love floating. Floating is easy and relaxing once you position your weight on your chest or back and engage your muscles so other parts of your body don't sink.

The hard part of swimming is effectively shifting your weight to swim rather than just float. You move around in the water by shifting your weight. Many animals swim, not with an arm or a fin, but primarily with their bodies. Dolphins, fish, snakes and people move their core muscles to swim in the water. Then, in addition to the core movement, people use hands, arms, feet and legs help propel their weight in the water. The challenge to moving your weight in the water, is that you become both the point to move from in the water and the form of propulsion.

Learn to position your body's weight to create a point to move from in the water. The upper torso (chest, side and back) works best. If your weight is centered or positioned at your chest, you can more easily move in the water. Consider your chest to be like the single wheel of a wheelbarrow which can move your weight efficiently. A wheelbarrow is efficient at moving weight. Weight on one pivot point can shift easily. In the water, you want to easily shift your weight for movement, or you will just be floating. For weight shifts in the water, position your weight on your upper chest or upper back and not your waist, like you position your weight on land. The problem with many people in the water is that they want to continue to position their weight at their waist so they sink at their hips. What a waste of a perfectly good waist and weight in the water.

When you pivot or position your weight on one part of your body, while moving the rest of your body in the water, you can go faster and have more weight moving forward. Compare that conceptually to spreading your weight out to float. A dolphin or a whale does not flatten out and disperse their weight to swim. Their weight moves from one pivot point to another pivot point in a rolling, waving manner.

Your legs and arms are not effective weight bearing tools in the water compared to your torso. The legs and arms are effective weight moving levers in the water though. Your arms and legs are like propellers on a boat and propellers are not for weight bearing. Propellers are for propulsion.

Like a wheelbarrow, it will help you to balance your weight one one point, the chest, while swimming freestyle. With your weight on your chest, you can roll left and right to see and breathe while your arms, shoulders, and back muscles move in the direction that you want to go. The legs can also help you move forward by moving, but they are a less efficient means of propulsion and not a good return on oxygen (ROO) when swimming long distances.

In freestyle, your wave like motion is side to side while forward. Much like a skater goes side to side and forward, go side to side and forward in freestyle.

Skating is a positive comparison to think of while swimming. With your hand positioned thumbs up while swimming, the pinky down side of your hand is the "blade" of your skate in the water. When the edge of your right hand slices into the water, to the outside of your right shoulder, your weight slices right too and becomes centered on your right chest during the glide. Then, when it is time to shift weight left, the left hand slices the water at your shoulder while the right hand changes its angle to go from gliding to digging into the water, much like a skate blade turns and digs the ice. Yet, we are getting ahead of the story here.

Position your weight at your chest by leaning.

A somewhat popular team building exercise is called the trust fall. A person leans until they start falling and then another person or others catch them for support. The exercise builds trust that you can lean on your friend and they will support you. With a two person trust fall, one person leans with their feet on the ground while the other person supports the falling person's upper torso ,back or chest.

The water will support you too, like your friend, if you let it. And, that support can be found at same point where you want to pivot your weight, your upper torso. Throughout your freestyle, backstroke and sidestroke swimming, you want to lean your weight on your upper chest, side, or back. On your chest, that is the area where your breast is and on the back where your shoulder blades are. That area is the wheel of your wheelbarrow where the body's weight will pivot throughout the swim. You don't want the weight to shift to your hips. Weight shifting to the hips is the number one weight bearing mistake that you can make swimming freestyle, sidestroke or backstroke.

The trust fall only works if the person falling keeps their core muscles engaged and doesn't give or bend at their hips. Think of this scenario. You are there ready to support your friend. They lean towards you and you have your hands on their back to support them. And suddenly, their hips give and they plop down on the ground.

Too many swimmers plop or "sit down" at some point when swimming. It's understandable, because when they are on land, their weight is centered at the hips. Yet, if you are centering your weight at your chest and then plop or sit down even a little when you roll for a breath of air, you begin sinking in the water.

For the trust fall, and swimming and your wheelbarrow in the water, to be effective, you must keep the core engaged. The frame of a wheelbarrow is strong. As are the levers or handles that work with the front wheel.

A tight, taut, stretched chain with many links is also engaged. If you can keep your muscles tight and linked from your chest to your legs, then you won't be sitting down or falling or sinking as you swim.

One way people work around not engaging the core and sitting while they swim is to use flippers. Flippers let you cheat the water. Obviously, they allow you to swim faster. Less obviously, but more importantly they can make up for not engaging your core muscles and positioning your weight on the chest. When a person takes the flippers off, they then find, that while their legs might be stronger, they still can't swim without flippers. They haven't worked their core, especially their lower core muscle below the belly button.

Another way to cheat the swim is to use a wetsuit. The buoyancy and structure of a wetsuit supports the body and helps the swimmer with a less than engaged core.

A remarkably good result of bearing the weight properly at your upper chest and upper back is that you can kick less while swimming. My kicking drills achieve several goals at one time. One of the goals is to end the need to kick while swimming. Some of the best distance swimmers that I know, and have seen, have nary a kick while swimming fast. What if you did not have to kick to swim? Imagine something like a pull buoy, supporting your legs while you swim. Most distance swimmers swim faster with a pull buoy to restrict kicking. The conclusion that you can draw from using a pull buoy is that kicking is not a good return on oxygen (ROO). Kicking done to compensate for not having the weight positioned at the chest, rather than propulsion, creates the poor return on oxygen spent. Trusting that the water will support your weight at your chest when your core is engaged, reduces the work that your legs will have to perform. This is an important benefit for a triathlete or distance swimmer.

Let's review what we have learned so far. The first thought, and this will become less conscious over time, is what and where are you going to see. The second thought is exhaling underwater. The third thought is leaning your weight on your chest, side or back when swimming freestyle, sidestroke, or backstroke.

With practice, these three actions will be come less of a conscious effort over time. Yet, no matter how good you are, you want to practice these three actions because they are pivotal to good swimming.

Chapter Four – Freestyle kicking

A swimmer's kick versus a runner's kick.

You can immediately see a runner's kick in someone else while swimming. The legs are behind them and moving backwards as if they were running in the water. The problem with the runner's kick is that the backward kick catches a lot of water and slows you down. In fact, it slows some people down so much that they go backwards while kicking on their backs in the water. (Note: injured runners could lay on their back and run in the water without buying a flotation device.)

So, if you "run" while swimming, you need to change from kicking backwards to kicking forwards. Think of the way you kick forward when kicking a ball. Or better yet, think of how people constantly kick forward when juggling a soccer ball or hacky sack in front of them. While the legs go back a little, the real focus is to get the legs back to front to keep the ball in the air or propel you in the water.

To create the swimmer's kick, you want to feel more water pressure on the front of your leg and foot. Feel more resistance forward while kicking. The resistance on the backside of your leg and foot will feel non-existent in comparison. It is a challenge getting your kick in front of your hips while swimming. While you can kick your leg in front of you on land, it is much harder to get your kick in front of you while swimming. Even swimmers trying to over exaggerate the forward kick, normally bring the kick only as far forward as their hips. Their bodies look straight in the water when kicking forward. Being straight in the water is what you want. A kick sticking out behind you, catching water, and creating drag you don't want.

Your kick will improve more by kicking on your back while kicking against gravity.

Many people do their kicking with a kick board, kicking downwards. A coach for young swimmers said that the main benefit of the kick board is that swimmers can talk to one another during a workout so they don't get bored with the workout. I would have to agree. With my approach though, it is better to practice kicking in the same position that you find yourself swimming, with your head in the water. No visiting and talking during a practice? Well, kids can have their kick boards so they can talk and visit during a workout.

Kicking downwards is easier than kicking upwards. Lying on the floor face down and kicking downwards is easier than lying face up on your back while kicking upwards. When you kick downwards, it requires less effort and less core muscle engagement. If you stay with kicking upward while lying on your back, you may notice that your core abdominal and back muscles tire before your legs. Increasing your core muscle strength for a strong frame to maintain your weight at your chest is one of your kicking goals, too.

Another goal is a forward kick. Kicking face down or downward does not really address or fix the backward kick. It hides it. Kicking from your side or back fixes the runner's kick because you must start kicking forward or you go nowhere. You develop better kicking technique while kicking on your back. The time you spend on your back during kicking drills is actually more valuable, than face down kicking. I recommend that you spend half of the time on your back and half of the time face down while doing kicking drills. The additional effort that you experience on your back will bring about the gains you want in a forward kick and core strength faster than face down kicking.

You can go from a runner's kick to a swimmer's kick to an optional kick.

If you are a small person you probably want to kick. For a small swimmer, a kick helps keep momentum going in between strokes. On the other hand, from the moment, I saw big Jim Stewart not kicking as he swam, I wanted a "non-existent" kick like his. I could hardly tell the difference between Jim Stewart with a pull buoy to hold up his legs and Jim without one. Jim has been, for several years now, a national age group champion in the United States Masters Swimming (USMS).

As a triathlete, you may want to save your legs for the bike or the run. A larger swimmer with mass does not slow down as much in between strokes so kicking for propulsion is less of an issue. If you weigh less than 150 pounds, you might want to keep kicking though. If you weigh over 150 pounds, you could kick less if your technique is good. As a swim instructor, I can get big men, who look like bowling balls in the water, below a ten stroke count for twenty five yards without kicking. On the other hand though, small women and children need to kick to get below ten strokes for twenty-five yards. As a triathlete on the border line, my preference is not to kick. Seconds of time lost in the water can more easily be made up in the air, or on land, than in the thicker water.

Kicking is optional once you know where and how to position your weight.

The key to not kicking is proper weight bearing at the chest, on your side and on your back with your core engaged. To learn how to kick less, begin by kicking more slowly. Kicking or swimming slowly forces you to better position your weight where it needs to be to avoid sinking. One of my favorite challenges to a swim team or a workshop of swimmers is to see who can swim a length slowest. Poor swimmers have to go faster so they don't sink. Good swimmers can go slower.

Once you are kicking slowly, learn to make a kick like motion only when the opposite hand enters the water. This is like your walking motion. When your right hand goes forward, your left foot goes forward too. This might feel like a pair of scissors centered on its screw. As the thumb pushes down, the scissor blade comes up.

41

You will also find it easier to initially stop kicking after you inhale. After you inhale and you throw your arm forward, you can stop your kick without loss of momentum.

It is more of a challenge to stop kicking while inhaling until you learn how to position your weight. It's a common mistake to kick more when rolling for air to compensate for your weight shifting to your hips.

ROO (return on oxygen)

Whether you are a big swimmer or a small swimmer, a kick is generally not a good return on oxygen. Yes, I have seen swimmers let their kicks rip and they swim quite fast. Yet, they are the first swimmers to tire. The swimmers barely kicking seldom have to stop for air and rest.

The leg muscles are big muscles that use up a disproportionate amount of oxygen compared to the arms, shoulders, back or core muscles while swimming. And, the lungs can not differentiate where the oxygen burn occurs. The lungs only know that they are losing the battle and the entire body will have to slow down because the legs overspent their share of the oxygen. That is a poor return on oxygen (ROO).

Use the proper muscle groups for the sport. While runners who sprint receive a short term advantage from pumping their arms faster and harder to sprint, distance runners don't work their arms nearly as much. Distance runners want their arms to glide along for the run. If we added a hand and arm mechanism to a bicycle, the return on oxygen from our arm strength, would not be worth it.

So while the kicking drills are challenging, focus on weight positioning while strengthening the core to improve your forward kicking technique so you kick efficiently or hardly kick at all.

Chapter Five– Freestyle hands and arms.

Your hands and arms determine what your body will be like.

One of the most important concepts that differentiates these techniques is the emphasis on your hands and arms. It is hard for your body to do any better than your hands and arms. Yet, if you get your hands and arms correct, the body seems to correct itself, too.

If your elbow is bent in front of you, your hips are going to bend, especially when you roll for a breath of air. If you arms are not straight in front of your shoulders, you will find it hard to swim straight. If you leave your hand flat in the water when you roll for air, your body will not roll as well and you will begin your catch and pull (row) before you normally would when not rolling for air. Many swimmers take a bad stroke when inhaling because their hands are flat in the water and the shoulder will defend itself from the impingement. The last thing that you need when trying to inhale is a bad stroke that is shorter than the other strokes that you take.

The palm of the hand, your forearm, your elbow and your upper arm represent your head, your torso, your waist and your lower body accordingly. Even on land, you will find it easier if your palm and face are facing in the same direction rather than opposite directions. On land, you can also stand and feel how straightening your arm at your elbow by reaching also straightens your hip making your body more streamlined too. When you get your hands and arms correct, there is a chain reaction throughout the body that helps you correct the mistakes that the body might otherwise make.

Your arms do more than propel you. Your arms set the tone for your body. It now becomes a conscious or unconscious decision as to how well you will use your arms to set the tone for your body and your swim. If you choose bent elbows and a scrunched up swim, that is what you will get. If you choose long, straight arms and swimming with extension, that is what you will get. If you streamline your hands and arms, your body will be streamlined. It's difficult for your body to be better than your hands and arms while swimming. Use your arms to set the tone, direction and help position your weight before you use them to propel yourself. "Dog paddlers" make the mistake of using their arms to propel themselves without considering how much more their hands and arms could help them in other ways.

Your hands and arms can help orient the body.

The hands are powerful orientation tools. Whether walking, skating, dancing, or swimming, the hands lead the body. The hands and arms provide orientation that the body follows.

Even in the water the hands and arms make poor feet and legs. The hands and arms are not as good for weight bearing and there is no solid surface with much friction to bear the weight. Therefore, use the hands to do what they do really well, which is, set the direction and tone for the body to follow.

Whatever you want your body to do, have your hand and arm do it first. If you want your body to go forward, your hands lead you forward. If you want your body to turn, your hands lead the turn. When you want to roll of air, your hand leads the roll. When your body is at forty-five degrees gliding on your left side while swimming, your left hand arrived first and remains at a forty-five degree angle until you row. Like a dancer or a skater or a walker who uses their hands to lead their bodies, you use your hands and arms to lead your body while swimming. When you see awkward swimmers you notice that the hands are leading the body awkwardly.

Your hand and arm will take you from wheelbarrow to wagon.

In the kicking drills and while swimming, employing the hands and arms makes swimming much easier. The difference in ease can be compared to using a wagon rather than a wheelbarrow. It is much easier to take the handle of a wagon and balance and direct a wagon, than direct and balance a wheelbarrow. Consider your extended hand and arm to be a handle. Your body is the wagon. With a handle in front of the wagon, being stretched forward, it's easy to direct and move the wagon. The handle is turned left to move the wagon left. The handle is turned right to move the wagon right. The handle is an effective lever on the wagon.

To roll your body, your wagon, to air, train the handle to lead the roll rather than stay flat in the water and resist the body's roll for air. Roll your hand to air and your body will want to follow it too. Keep your hand flat or thumbs down and you are putting your hand and body, at the rotator cuff, at odds with what your body is doing.

45

Swim with a body lean to the left side and then right side and back and forth while swimming. Have your hand lead the back and forth motion and the angle of the lean. If you want to lean at forty-five degrees, like many people do, have your hand at forty-five degrees. Swimmers really are flat in the water only when rolling from one side to the other. When swimming on the left side, the left hand and body are both at a forty-five degree angle for better performance.

Pendulum clocks work well swinging back and forth. Forty-five degrees to one side and then forty-five degrees to the other works well. It's natural to have that range as you swim. The body will want to mirror and follow the hand. That is good. Do not fight the mirroring. Use mirroring to your advantage. It is much easier to position your hand rather than your entire body.

You can strive to have your handle leading your body or you can swim like pushing a wheelbarrow. Not having an arm in front of you, is like walking or running with hands and arms at your sides. Yet, some people make that mistake while swimming.

Swimming begins in front of your body. Your hand and arm set the tone for the body. Your arm in front of you stakes out your place, and where you are going, and where you want to be in the water. Your arm got there first and your body is going there next.

As triathletes, when someone is in front of us swimming, we want to be touching the feet in front of us with our hands and not our head. If you are too close and a competitor kicks you in the head knocking your goggles off, they will think that it was your fault for being to close. It was. If you are close and touching their feet with your hand, they will think you are going to be pass them. You could.

Keeping a hand in front also increases speed by keeping you level, streamlined and maintaining momentum. A reaching hand and arm creates a tautness and line that the body follows. Good reaching engages the entire body in the reach. Exaggerating the reach streamlines the body and is propulsive.

Again, the body mirrors the hand and arm. Your hand represents your head. Your forearm your torso. Your elbow your hip. Your upper arm your leg. For example: if your elbow is straight and reaching, your hips straighten and reach too.

The good news here is that control begins with your hands and arms. You can set the tone for your entire body through hand and arm movement while swimming.

In the dynamics of hand and arm movements, consider the swim to be a combination of THROWS AND ROWS. You want a high quality throw that your body will follow. And, you want a high quality row that happens after the throw enters the water. Like a baseball pitcher, focus on the throw first. Throw and row splits the workload and is much easier than ROW, ROW, ROW. More on this later.

A safe position for your shoulder is when your hand, arm and chest roll together.

Unfortunately, rotator cuff injuries are a common occurrence among swimmers. I think many swimmers develop rotator cuff injuries from planting the hand flat when rolling or turning the other way. While final "injury" may occur away from swimming, while lifting weights for example, the cause of the injury came from repetitive trauma of the rotator cuff while swimming.

Rotator cuff injuries amongst swimmers can also occur when you reach the end of the pool and hold the wall while turning. If you hold the desk or something in front of you with your hand flat and turn your body, you will feel the impingement in the shoulder. Avoid holding the pool wall and turning at the same time. Do a right side up flip turn instead.

While swimming with a flat hand and rolling for air, you have hurt the shoulder in a similar way. Your hand remained stationary while your body turned and your shoulder is pinched. Do this several thousand times in a swim and you can have shoulder and rotator cuff problems.

One way that the body tries to protect your shoulder is to have you begin your underwater part of your stroke, the row, early in order to bring the arm back to your side. When the hand and arm come back earlier than your normal stroke while breathing, it's your body taking the strain off of your shoulder, so you don't hurt the shoulder even more. However, your performance suffers when your stroke is a one handed row. The glide portion of the inhale is over. The stroke is inferior to your non-inhaling strokes and you are not in position for the THROW BEFORE YOU ROW for your next stroke.

The swim coaches are slowly going from thumbs down to a flatter hand. Thumbs down hand entries were once, and still are in some places, the norm. It is a challenge to get someone who was taught thumbs down to try thumbs up. If they were willing to try thumbs down, why not try thumbs up.

It is difficult to interpret what you are really seeing when you watch an athlete perform. Your eyes can fool you and there are many parts that influence the one result that you are seeing. For example, I guess the thumb could look "down" as the hand passes the shoulder on the way to your waist in the pull or row part of the stroke. When your body is moving in a multidimensional way, it is easy to misinterpret what is happening. Some coaches have moderated to a flat hand approach. I think some of the remaining logic behind the flat had is that most think a flat hand is a better hand position to row or catch and pull the water.

I teach that the hand can go from an angled thumbs up position to a flat hand while rowing or in a drumming like motion down and back to the thigh while swimming.

What I like about our results is that the glides during the inhales last longer regardless of your flexibility. The hand is still in front of the swimmer ready for the THROW BEFORE THE ROW without the shoulder impingement. The head is protected with the arm leading. The body stays streamlined longer. We look better, too.

So when you push off from the wall in the pool, as a triathlete, have your hands and arms as far apart as your shoulders and in front of your shoulders like a catamaran. Hands and arms touching together like a torpedo is bad form for a distance swimmer as you retain that muscle memory for the remainder of the length. Have catamaran hands and arms or your stroke will remember the torpedo and continue to cross in front of you while you swim.

When swimming, think of where you are going to look or see. Second, get the underwater exhale going. Third, your weight positioned on your upper torso. And fourth, an arm in front of you that leads the body.

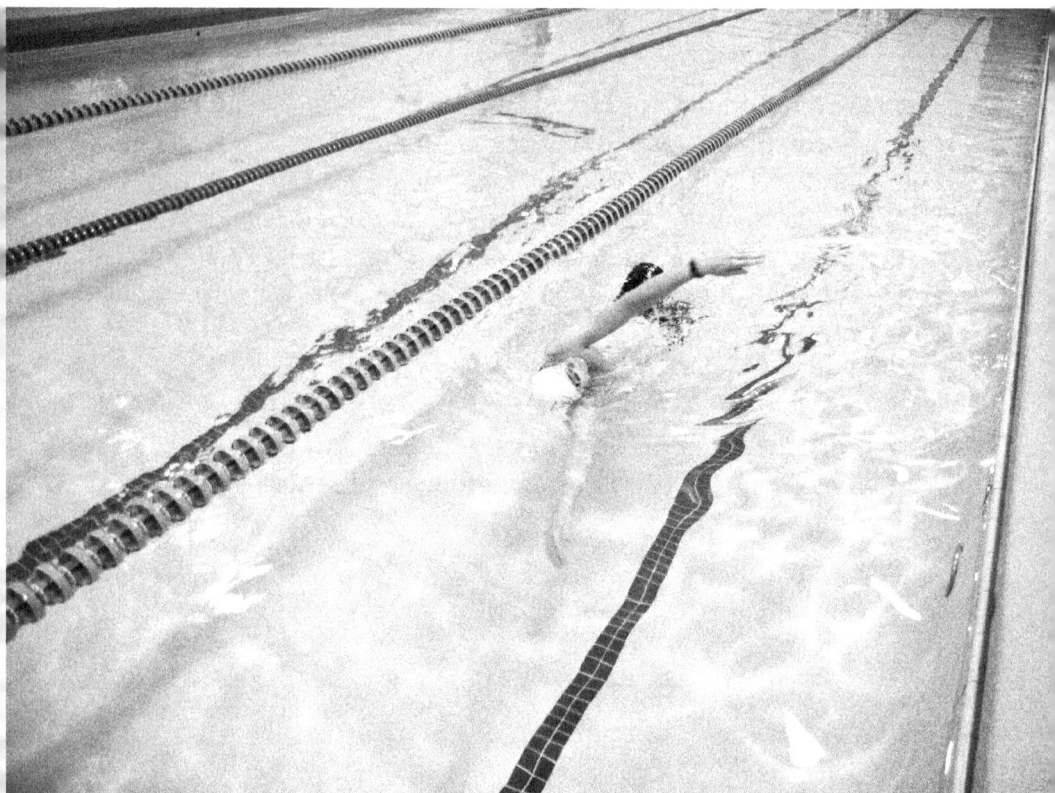

Chapter Six – Transferring and propelling your weight

Swimming is weight transfer.

You transfer your own weight better with your arms straight in front of your shoulders as compared to your arms close to you. As you sit or stand, extend both arms and reach as far as they possibly can. Move the arms back and forth to transfer your body's weight. Then, pull both arms back to body. Move the arms close to your body back and forth to transfer your weight. Hopefully, you discover that your body rolls and moves and transfers more weight with more power with outstretched arms.

A quality throw reaches maximum extension below the water.

A throw that straightens your arm and goes immediately, directly, and forcefully to the point of the "catch" or row is what you want. Don't be lackadaisical or fainthearted with the easiest part of propulsion. Some people swim with either a slow, tentative throw or an indirect throw which slows them down. Consider that your hand and arm is moving through the thin air while the rest of you is in a liquid a hundred times thicker. Have your hand and arm go fast through the air where it is easiest to pick up some speed, force, and time. For economy in propulsion, go fast where it is easiest to go fast.

A throw that does not extend the arm, leaving the elbow bent, is not going to be a strong throw. A reason that many people do not throw well is because they mistakenly think that an arm in front of the head creates more streamline for the body. The bent arm then contributes to the row, row, row. They incorrectly have not developed an athletic throw to power their swim with their body's weight. An arm bent at the elbow does get a person rowing underwater sooner. Yet, it is much harder to move your hand in the water than in the air. And, the hand in the water is doing most of the work, alone. Many people do view a swim stroke as one underwater pull or one row after the other. Fewer people see the stroke as the throw and the row working in unison so a stroke becomes the work of two hands and arms and not just one hand and arm taking turns at the work.

Many swimmers throw and land their stroke at water level as far forward as they can reach in the air. While I like the idea of moving the arm through the air, it is more efficient to simply drop your body's weight in the water rather than extend the weight drop. You want to throw and land your stroke sooner, deeper at what feels to be your shoulder. In some ways, the throw is like landing a punch or blow. You are not going to punch very well if you are punching high above your head.

People generally do not stack shelves by getting as close to the wall as possible while stacking it overhead. A better angle would be stacking the shelves in front of you where you can see what you are doing and have a better angle. The angle is also like climbing a ladder. A ladder that is positioned straight up the wall has your arms reaching above your head and is harder to climb than a ladder that is angled towards a wall. Do not swim with your arms above your head. Swim with your forearm angled and going into the water sooner rather than later.

After the throw, you can keep your glide and streamlined body going by extending the arm outstretched. Keep your arm extended waiting for the other arm's throw to come back in front. The trick to this for most people is keeping the arm extended in front and not prematurely rowing. This is similar to playing defense in basketball where you want to keep an arm up to defend and block a basketball shot. The hand and arm is always there fully extended to stop the shot. And, when you need to switch arms playing basketball, your arm stays extended until the other arm takes it place.

You are positionally at your best when your arm is fully extended at the end of the throw. A good throw helps you achieve maximum propulsion during the stroke cycle. After the throw, you are at your most streamlined position for the glide. And then, you want your leading arm to remain in a gliding position, like a skater on one skate, until the other arm arrives in front of that shoulder to replace it in front of you. You want a hand and arm always leading you.

You can row in freestyle like you are beating a drum.

Most people can already row when they swim. Some better than others. The row propels the body by digging into the water. When your hand and arm are flat, like an oar or a paddle, in the water you are rowing. Rowing the water is not easy though. As your hands and arms tire, it's easy to start tilting your hand and arm so they angle or slip in the water, while rowing, which reduces the effectiveness of the row. On land, if you had to lift ten or twenty pounds, with one arm over and over more than a thousand times, your technique would drop off and the quality of the lift suffers.

If you are rowing a boat or paddling a canoe, you often start out with the blade flat and pulling or rowing. As you tire, the blade becomes less and less flat because it's hard to keep the same stroke rate and stroke force. So while angling the blade allows you to keep rowing at the same rate, your rowing becomes less effective because the blade of the oar is slipping ever so slightly in the water. Along this line of thought, you really don't want your underwater row to speed up just for the sake of moving fast. Moving fast could mean that the underwater row is not resisting, catching or rowing the water as effectively in order to propel you. You don't want your hand and arm slipping underneath you in the water. You want a quality row.

What works well for rowing technique is taking your hand and arm from their full extension at the end of the throw to your chest and waist in a flat handed drum beating motion. Imagine your hand hitting a flat bongo or conga drum at your waist with force. That flatness and force without much of an angle to the hand, would make for a good row.

Like lifting a weight dozens of times with the same motion, it's easy for your technique to go from good to poor. For example, your first twenty pushups look great. Yet, your last twenty pushups lack the same quality. This happens with your swim stoke. To prevent this from happening, I am going to help you improve your focus and provide you with some alternatives to give your muscles a break while you swim.

You throw before you row.

To break the habit of row, row, row, you learn to delay the row until the throw arrives on the scene, in front of its shoulder. Imagine yourself at a kitchen counter trying to get something from the top cupboard that is beyond your reach. You place one hand and arm on

53

the counter ready to push down and steady you. You have the other hand and arm ready to reach up to the top shelf which is is just out of reach when you jump. You thrust your hand and arm upward while pushing down on the counter in order to get that can from the cupboard. Just pushing down on the cupboard would not have gotten the can.

Throw before you row splits the propulsive work making both actions easier and faster. One hand and arm begins the propulsion forward with a throw, a reach, a punch or a slingshot while the other hand and arm shares and completes the propulsion with a good flat push off, pull or row. Just rowing or just throwing doesn't work as well. You need to do both to swim like you walk, run or skate. When walking, running, or skating the foot remains on the ground until the foot and leg that you are throwing moves forward. Only after the forward movement of your foot and leg, does your other foot and leg plant to push off. Swim like you run

Hopefully, the first four thoughts are becoming automatic requiring less of your attention: see, exhale, weight positioned and arm in front. The fifth thought is throw before you row with every stroke.

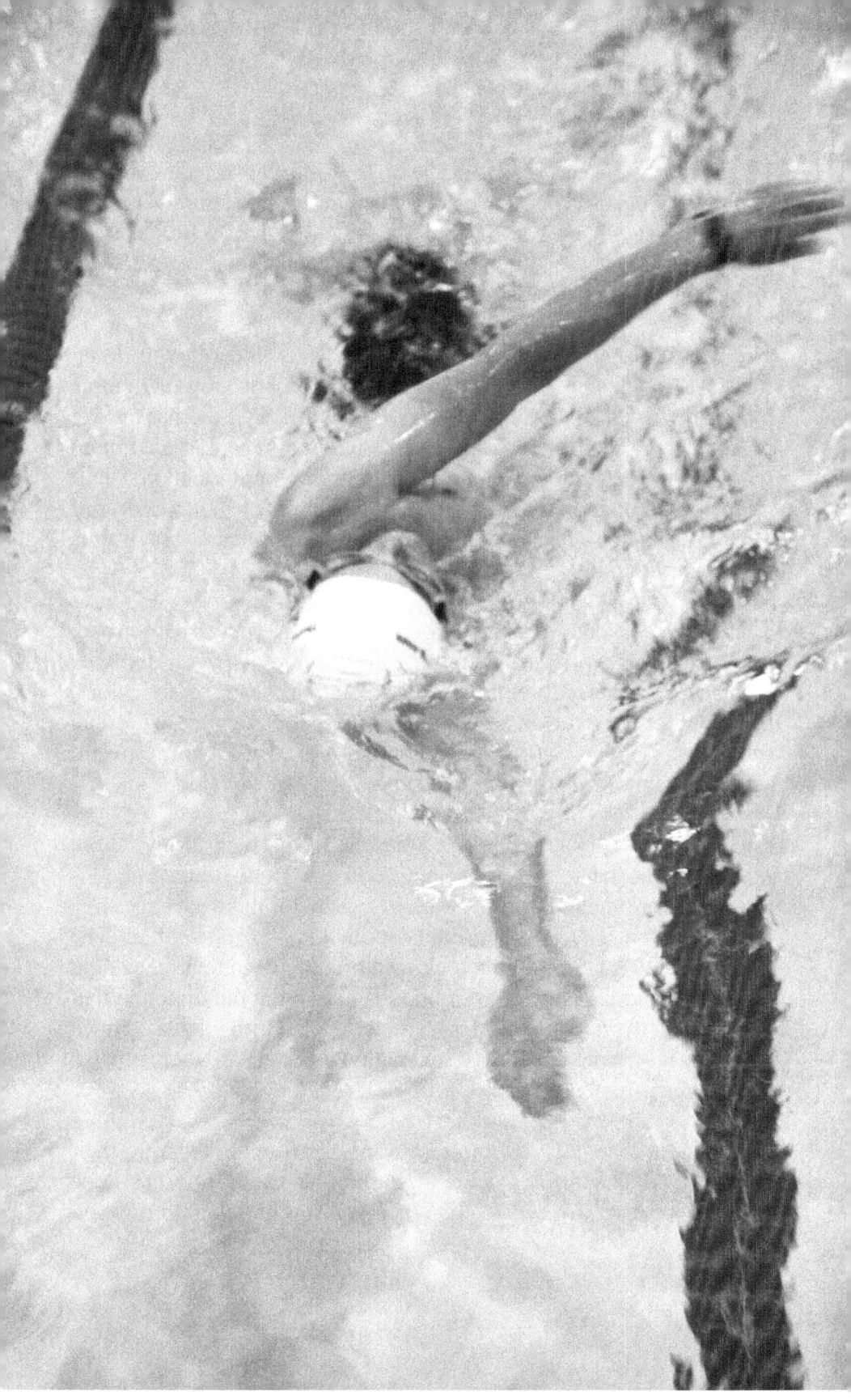

Chapter Seven – Backstroke

There are two versions of backstroke. Both have value to the triathlete. One protects the head well. One is like doing jumping jacks while laying on your back in the water. Both backstrokes keep your face out of the water pretty well, which is one reason why many people like to backstroke.

The backstroke that you see in the Olympics is like a downside up freestyle or upside down freestyle. A comparison of Olympic records between freestyle and backstroke tell us that the backstroke is about five seconds slower over one hundred meters at maximum speeds. Five seconds per hundred meters would amount to a half minute to a minute in most sprint triathlons. Some triathletes do roll to their backs for a backstroke break without significant loss of time during a triathlon.

There are several reasons to like the Olympic backstroke. Backstroke can work as a swimming drill to improve your freestyle. Backstroke builds and improves your kick more than freestyle does. Breathing is less of an issue. Backstroke stretches the back and shoulders. You increase your abdominal core by kicking upward against gravity while on your back and rolling side to side.

The timing of backstroke is like freestyle in that you throw before you row. The hand that is "resting" on the front of the thigh is thrown before the hand in the water rows. With this sequence, like freestyle, you have two propulsive actions at one time. The throwing action is one hundred percent propulsive in that the weight of the arm and that side of your body is moving in the direction that you want to go. The rowing action is also propulsive. Timed together, the throw and row divides the workload on your arms so backstroke is easier and faster.

Like freestyle, some swimmers want to row, row, row their backstroke. Their throws come after the one armed row has done much of the hard work by itself. When you row and then throw, you had the hard effort set up the easy effort which is backwards to how you want to work.

Throwing before you row has the economy of the easier effort through the air initiating the harder effort in the water. Olympic backstroke swimmers quickly have a hand and arm thrown above their shoulder. The hand and arm can travel much faster in the air and this is easy propulsion compared to the row in the water. Use your easy propulsion, in the air, to set up the harder propulsion in the water.

Add thumbs up technique.

The thumb is pointed up to the ceiling or sky as you swim on your back A thumb up or pinky down position creates an oar or blade for the rowing arm in the water. If you are not sure of what a thumbs up position would feel like, stand with one shoulder blade against a wall with your hand and arm straight above your shoulder with your little finger or pinky touching the wall. Hopefully, you felt the little finger down and the thumb pointed in the direction of your face as if you had been in the water. Perhaps even better, you could lie on the floor with your hand and arm straight above your shoulder with your little finger touching the floor, too. While on the floor, with little finger down, the thumb is certainly up.

As you throw the stroke in the air, have your thumb in up position so that your hand lands little finger down in the water. You don't want to take precious time and effort to reposition your hand in the water to effectively row. Your throw can be athletic. The throw can be similar to delivering a karate chop behind you. Your throw can also be a good stretch, as if the arm is stretching each vertebrae and back muscle on that side when it reaches straight up, straight back and just outside of your shoulder.

Often people make the mistake of throwing their hand and arm above their head rather than in front of their shoulder. Perhaps they can not feel the difference or the throw over your shoulder feels too wide when throwing the arm in backstroke or freestyle. On land, using a mirror so you can see your throw is helpful. You can see in a mirror if your forearm is directly over you head or over your shoulder so you can correct yourself.

Backstroke develops your kick.

It is harder to kick upward against gravity. Backstroke works your kick one hundred percent of the time against gravity. The kick in backstroke often accounts for more propulsion than freestyle kick does. Rather than using a kick board to improve your kick, do the backstroke to develop your kick. The backstroke develops a higher quality, tighter, forward kick. You won't go fast or far, if anywhere, if you keep a deep and wide, runner's kick in the water below and behind you while you are on your back. When you are kicking to the surface of the water, you are developing a strong forward kick while not allowing the kick to travel far below you. A tight, forward kick is also the kick that you want for freestyle and your freestyle drills.

Develop your core muscles.

Many swimmers are seated when swimming backstroke. When you look below the water's surface, it is as if they are sitting while swimming. Trying to sit while you swim is not efficient. Sitting creates more drag and you have to kick to avoid sinking further rather than kicking for propulsion.

Like freestyle's wheelbarrow position on the chest, you position your weight on one shoulder blade or scapula. With your weight positioned high on your upper back and lowest abdominal muscles below the navel engaged, you won't be seated. Your hips will lift and your effort lessens because your weight is correctly positioned. As you swim backstroke, your weight will transfer from one shoulder blade to the other shoulder blade. Your body will rotate forty-five degrees to the left and then right, like freestyle, while the head remains up, out of the water and stationery.

With your weight on your upper back, you can better develop your core muscles. Many people neglect or are not aware of their abdominal muscles below their belly button or navel. There is another set of abdominal muscles below the navel, that we seldom notice on land because we are working the upper abs when bending down or doing sit ups. The lowest set of abdominal muscles are used to lift the hips up. We seldom use these lower abdominal muscles because we are seldom on our backs lifting the hips up. Yet, these are important muscles to develop, because if you don't, this set of muscles become the weak link in your chain of core muscles. And, it only takes one weak link to lead to failure. In backstroke, the failure of the lowest core muscles leads to being seated at your hips. In freestyle, this same core failure leads to your hip giving or dipping when rolling for your inhale.

While other swim coaches allow swimmers at their workshops and swim lessons to use flippers, I do not. Flippers hide the weakness of the lower abdominal muscles by having an aided kick overcome a set of weak lower abs, the lack of forward kick and a lack of foot flexibility. Flippers hide or cover up your weaknesses and when you take them off, you still won't have what you need.

Stretching and strengthening the back and spine.

The backstroke is an integral part of my warmup and recovery swim. One-fourth of my time during warmup or recovery swim training is spent doing the backstroke. Do you want to feel a good back stretch and feel taller? As we get older, we lose height. Running does not help us retain height and that is why it is a good idea to swim your cool down with some backstroke after running. The backstroke stretches the spinal column when you throw before you row. A good, straight throw that reaches in the direction that you want to go stretches and strengthens the spine and the back muscles. However, just rowing your backstroke tends to shorten and scrunch your back on one side and then the other side.

The recovery that your back experiences is worth every stroke. Every stroke can be a stretching and strengthening movement. The slight additional water pressure that is on your back helps send blood from those muscles back to the heart for more oxygen and nutrients. The water safely allows you to stretch and strengthen your back.

When to use backstroke.

When you want to recover while swimming use your back stroke. Once your weight is positioned high on your upper back and off your hips, you are floating. If your weight is at your hips though, you will be sinking and will have to kick more which reduces the recovery effect.

Rather than treading water, use backstroke to make some progress in the water. Although slower than freestyle, backstroke is actually easier than treading water and you move in the direction you want to go. Treading water requires more energy than backstroke because you are displacing your weight over a smaller surface area. And, treading water during a triathlon is not a good idea. Treading water could be like parking on a freeway where no one is expecting you to stop. Don't plan on treading water if you need a break. Plan on doing the back stroke or breaststroke if you need to recover during a triathlon.

When you want to see the sky or the shore, use your backstroke. Seeing to your side or up is an improvement over not seeing anything when you are face down in murky water. When the sun is not a factor, you can consistently see for long uninterrupted periods with the backstroke.

You can use the backstroke when your freestyle muscles tire and break down. Any swim stroke is like lifting a weight a thousand times. It is natural that you would tire and your stroke lose its efficiency. Rather than continue to develop or get used to a low quality stroke, go to another style of swim stroke to rest tired arms.

Use backstroke when you need more air. Breathing is much less restricted during the backstroke. If you are out of breath and unable to swim freestyle, it better to catch your breath while making some progress in the water with your backstroke.

How to go from freestyle to backstroke to freestyle.

To alternate between swim strokes have your hands and arms in front of you when alternating or changing from freestyle to backstroke. When you want to go from freestyle to backstroke, THROW AND ROLL to your backstroke, like you will learn in the drills. Your thumbs up throw will facilitate your roll to air into a thumbs up, pinky down backstroke position.

Observers have remarked that a powerful throw and roll to the back seems even faster than normal freestyle speed. It could be. The movement is similar to a high jumper doing the Fosbury flop over the high jump bar. This kind of high jump has you facing the bar in your run-up and then leading with your hand and arm as you suddenly turn your back to the bar and go over the high jump bar on your back. That "screwy" turn is a very propulsive maneuver in the air and in the water.

While swimming, it is always a good idea for the hand and arm to be leading the body. The easy propulsion of the freestyle throw sets up your roll to backstroke. From your backstroke position, you will continue to throw and then row to have the easy propulsion set up the harder propulsion and protect your head.

When you are ready to go back to freestyle from the backstroke, THROW AND ROLL down into freestyle swimming.

At every level, whatever you want your body to do, you will find it easier if your hands and arms do it first.

Elementary backstroke

The jumping jacks of swimming.

Perhaps the easiest stroke, for people comfortable on their backs, is the elementary backstroke. The elementary backstroke is floating with a jumping jack like leg and arm movement to move your body. Some master swimmers over eighty use the elementary backstroke in competition because it is the fastest stroke they have.

Elementary backstroke technique usually requires less teaching of technique than any of the other strokes. Yet, some people do get the technique wrong or do not optimize the stroke. The stroke has some benefit for developing you as a swimmer. Some benefits are that the elementary backstroke is a good recovery stroke. You can develop your breaststroke kick with less strain to the medial meniscus and medial ligaments at the knee. You engage the entire core and hold the core muscles while gliding after the jumping jack action. And, your foot tends not to cramp like it could on your back with a flutter kick.

Techniques for two types of elementary backstroke.

One technique for elementary backstroke is when the hands and arms do not come out of the water. The hands and arms start at your side and sneak up your side. The hands go outward and then your hands and arms row back to your sides. If your hands and arms do not sneak up and out and away from the body more gently than your rowing action, the throwing action in the water offsets some of the rowing action.

A second technique for elementary backstroke has the hands and arms leaving the water. Both arms are thrown at the same time over your shoulders and in the direction you want to go. This second technique is somewhat like an upside down butterfly stroke. Like butterfly, be prepared for your face to go under the water when your arms are above your head. Archimedes principle is true that when you move or add some weight above the surface of water, the boat sinks proportionately.

With all backstroke arm movements, the hands are thumbs up through out the stroke so that the movement is shoulder neutral with hands and arms in position to row.

The timing of your kick is different between the two elementary backstrokes. When keeping your hands and arms in the water, do your jumping jack kick at the same time as your hand and arms move. When throwing your hands and arms out of the water, the kick is slightly before the throwing action of the arms to create the easier propulsion first. With the second technique for elementary backstroke, the kick is stage one propulsion, the out of the water throwing action is stage two, and stage three is the in the water power row with both arms. Combine these three stages and hold your core tight for a long glide and you may have a stroke that could be as fast as your freestyle stroke.

I did discover, the hard way, a safety problem with the elementary backstroke. One morning, I rammed my head into the pool wall nearly giving myself a concussion and hurting my neck. The main problem with the elementary backstroke is that it leaves the head unprotected.

With thumps up swimming and my emphasis on throw before you row, your head is protected by a leading hand and arm with the other swim strokes. Unfortunately, your head leads the body and your head is unprotected while doing the elementary backstroke. Hence the risk of bumping your head on the wall of the pool or something else in the open water with the elementary backstroke.

I do practice and do some swimming with the arms out of the water elementary backstroke to warm up my legs for the more demanding breaststroke kick and for my recovery. Use this stroke before doing breaststroke because the kicking action is similar to the breaststroke with only a third of the effort. The elementary backstroke kick is a good warmup to avoid medial meniscus strain. I also use it to teach full and prolonged core engagement after the kick and row, or jump.

Use the elementary backstroke for recovery, too. The elementary backstroke uses different muscles in different ways than the other strokes. If your freestyle muscles are tired, the elementary backstroke is the furthest stroke movement from what you had been doing. To stay fresh during freestyle performance drills, do a freestyle performance drill for a pool length followed by backstroke or breaststroke for a pool length. A complete recovery will allow you to be fresh for the more demanding freestyle techniques. And, you can recover better laying down on your back rather than standing at the end the pool.

Use the backstroke to reinforce core engagement and glide. After you take a stroke, hold the glide a little longer than normal. Learning how to lengthen your glide in this way, is also learning to engage the core without going to a seated position.

I am reluctant to recommend the elementary backstroke in the open water though. You could hit your head on something you can't see or feel. Even in the pool, you need to be conscious when approaching the pool wall. When in doubt, switch to the Olympic backstroke or another stroke as you near the wall so your throw before your row protects your head.

Chapter Eight – Breaststroke

It's said that twenty percent of the population can naturally do the breaststroke. Eighty percent of the people seem to struggle with the timing, kick and hand movements. Once you do have a good breaststroke, you can see straight ahead, exhale and inhale more easily than freestyle and protect yourself well from other swimmers in the open water with your breaststroke.

If you are part of the twenty percent, let's try to maximize what is already working well for you. If you are part of the eighty percent, let's break the breaststroke down into its parts and reconstruct the breaststroke for you in a certain order.

Breaststroke techniques have changed.

The breaststroke has gone from taking many strokes per length to taking fewer strokes per length. Today's breaststroke is more about face down gliding time in the water rather than face out of the water movement. However, because people like to see and breathe, taking many strokes per length still persists with beginners.

The breaststroke has also gone from a hard row back to your sides to keeping your hands in front of you. The problem with a deep row back to your sides is returning the hands and arms in front of you underwater without offsetting much of the propulsion that the row backwards created. Nowadays, you scull just enough to come up for air with little backward arm movement.

While sculling, your focus is to go from thumbs up to flat hand sculling to enhance the sculling movement. Sculling is like getting up on ice, you want a little movement to get yourself up, because a lot of movement is counterproductive. A scull is also like a slight of hand magic trick with your hands that you want to hurry so others don't see what your hands did. The faster you can complete the scull, the greater the water pressure under your hands and forearms is creating more lift for your chest and head while also getting back to the kick and glide faster.

In the breaststroke and freestyle, flat hands tend to rise up and out of the catch or scull position, therefore don't have flat hands as you glide. With your hands in catamaran position, your hands will not rise in the water unintentionally during the glide. You do want your hands to flatten to raise you during the sculling action.

Thumbs up hand positions catamaran your swim strokes and have your hands and arms in the ready to go position. As an open water swimmer and triathlete, be conscientious of the opportunity to switch to breaststroke or backstroke for performance benefits. With hands and arms in front, you keep your continuity and momentum because your stroke changes occur in front of you.

Your head and back can also help your sighting and inhale by arching for air. Some swimmers can "turtle" the head from below the water to out of the water without sculling because they have good flexibility in their back and neck.

The shallow, head down dive with each breaststroke.

Today's breaststroke is not about keeping the head out of the water. Keeping your head out of the water restricts a shallow, propulsive, dolphin style dive into the water with each stroke. While you might want to keep your head continually out of the water to see and breathe without restriction, you are sacrificing speed, energy and ultimately comfort, too.

Today's breaststroke for open water swimmers and triathletes is about a quick look, a quick inhale and shallow dive. The slowest part of the breaststroke is when you come up for air. You want to minimize the inhale and maximize the long, gliding exhale for best overall speed. The breaststroke kick is a very propulsive kick, yet coming up and out of the water ends the propulsion from your kick.

Two thirds or more of your propulsion in breaststroke comes from your legs. Completely closing your legs effectively for propulsion is important. Unfortunately, this is a problem area for some swimmers because they don't even realize that their legs are not coming together at the end of the kick. Sometimes it is easier to understand what the breaststroke kick can be by standing in the water and moving your hands and arms together in front of you. A clapping motion of the hands and arms in the water demonstrates how much water can be moved away from you. A great deal of water can be ejected for propulsion when the hands and arms come together completely. When you stop the hands and arms wide and keep them apart you are not allowing them to touch and you move less water. If you have one hand and arm, scissoring higher or lower than the other hand and arm, they miss each other and eject less water too.

Using the kick of the elementary backstroke helps develop your breaststroke kick. More people on their backs tend to bring the legs completely together. More people also scissor their kick less while on their back. The effort of your breaststroke kick, done on your back, is less than the face down breaststroke kick. The fact that the kick requires less force on the back may make it easier to get your technique right first on your back and then on your chest, face down in in the water.

It's all about timing.

The timing is not natural for most people when they start. You scull and breathe. You lower yourself back under the water with a shallow dive as you kick and glide. Repeat. The breaststroke is a sequence of events. If the timing was put to music think of eighth note scull and breathe, eighth note lower and the kick and glide being longer than a whole note or eight eighth notes. Try to make the glide eight times as long the inhale or kick.

Trying to go faster does not improve your timing. If I had a dollar for every beginner who tries to do something better by just trying to do it faster, I would have an unending source of revenue. It is a mistake to think that if you put the scull, dive and kick quickly together somehow the timing comes together. Many a brand new drummer tries playing faster (and louder) to improve their timing much to the chagrin of the rest of the family.

Going slower helps you discover the feel and timing. You want to feel the weight transfers and tipping points. Feeling the beat and effect of each movement helps you discover the timing. Slowly do several kicks. Slowly arch up for air and then down for gliding. Slowly scull and breathe.

Start with the feel and the timing of the breaststroke kick. Doing one, two or three kicks without any sculling or breathing and then standing in the pool allows you to feel the kick. Hurrying the three kicks, one right after the other, slows you down and does not allow a glide for distance. Three well spaced out kicks while holding your core in a plank position increases your overall speed and distance.

The legs can try to "kneel" horizontally to the surface and your feet come up behind your rear when you are face down. The legs then spread up, out and wide (and wider is better). The legs then slowly and completely close together. Repeat. Adding a breath of air right now could be counterproductive and overload. If you have just done the kick right, or wrong, you probably want to feel another one for more physical feedback.

After slowly feeling two or three kicks, your underwater exhale is probably close to being over. Come up for air. Inhale and lower or drop yourself back down in the water for another two kicks. Kick and glide. Slow your kicks down so that the movements are distinct to you. If your movements are not distinct and noticeable, you can not improve them.

You want to create a jump like the jump of the elementary backstroke or a jump in the air. When your timing is right, each stroke will feel like a horizontal dive or jump in the water. A visual image could be that of a basketball player with legs spread to box out their opponent and then they bring the legs together to jump and get the ball. The propulsion comes from your legs. The better your jumping action, the faster you will go.

Using breaststroke to sight.

Looking straight forward to see with the breaststroke is easier than looking straight forward with freestyle. Looking forward in freestyle is not part of the normal stroke action; whereas, looking forward in breaststroke is part of the stroke.

A huge benefit is the variability of how much you can see with breaststroke. In waves or a group of swimmers, you can scull and arch higher than you normally would to lift more of your upper body out of the water. You don't have to stay with a quick look and breath. You can increase your lift out of the water to look over people and look further over the water to scout out opportunity.

Using breaststroke to rest and catch your breath.

Another benefit, is that the breaststroke uses a different set of muscles than freestyle. Changing to the breaststroke to sight and breathe for a few seconds allows the freestyle muscles to take a break. In the pool, you become used to wall as a break or rest in your swim. In the open water, you can use your breaststroke to create a planned rest or break.

You can also measure your swim in the open water with freestyle strokes and breaststrokes. If twenty-five yards in the pool is made up of ten freestyle strokes and two breaststrokes, then ten freestyle strokes followed by two breaststrokes could be a good sequence, for measuring purposes, for you in the open water. Like the pool, you will have created for yourself a rhythm, rest and sighting routine, in the open water. Making certain that you are still on course is a large part of your open water strategy.

Using breaststroke to get other swimmers off your feet.

It's pretty common for other swimmers to be on your feet or close to you in an open water swim or triathlon. If another swimmer is touching or bumping you, doing a few powerful breaststroke kicks could have them backing off quickly.

Using others swimming the breaststroke for your orientation in the water.

When swimming in open water triathlons, you can also orient yourself based on swimmers who are swimming with a breaststroke. If you see someone doing the breaststroke, your odds are high that they are seeing where they are going and their body is pointing in the correct direction. If you swim parallel to someone who is breast-stroking, you are on the same course that they are on without having to do the breaststroke to sight for yourself. I would sooner trust the direction that someone is breast-stroking towards than the direction that someone is free-styling towards in a triathlon.

World record breaststroke time compared to freestyle.

The world record for 100 meter breaststroke is fifty-five seconds and freestyle is forty-five seconds. So the breaststroke is ten seconds slower per 100 meters. While ten seconds per hundred yards difference may sound significant, it would amount to less than one minute in a sprint triathlon, if you went the entire distance with breaststroke.

When to use your breaststroke.

If a ten second difference of breaststroke accomplishes either one of these two goals: keeps you on course and/or gives your freestyle muscles a break, it is worth switching to some breaststroke in an open water swim.

No one is awarded time bonuses for style or sticking with freestyle so be strategic and tactical when swimming. Go from one swim stroke to another to stay on course and give your muscles a break. There is nothing so fatiguing as discovering that you are off course while swimming and having to swim back. One of your highest priorities in the swim is to stay on course and not turn a six hundred yard swim into a seven hundred yard swim by swimming off course. Sight as often as you need to stay on course and give your muscles a two or three breaststroke break.

Time yourself to find your best combination of freestyle strokes to breaststroke. My swimmers have varied from four freestyle strokes and four breaststrokes to ten freestyle strokes and two breaststrokes. Time yourself over one hundred yards or more. You may find you actually lose no time when you get the combination right.

How to go from freestyle to breaststroke to freestyle.

Remember that all changes from one stroke to another happen in front of you. Your hands lead the change in front of you and the body will follow.

Your freestyle stroke becomes breaststroke when you keep the leading hand and arm in front and your other hand and arm catches up with it in front of you. As I write this, I think of the freestyle drill that is called the catch up drill where you do just that action, one hand catches up with the other in front of you. While I don't recommend the catch up drill for freestyle, that would be what you want here for the transition from freestyle to breaststroke. Let both hands catch up with both hands in front of you.

Once both hands are in front, you scull, sight, inhale, shallow dive, and then kick and glide. You may want one to four breaststrokes to accomplish your goals of sighting and giving yourself a break. If you are weak at the breaststroke, take fewer strokes and not more. If your breaststroke is as fast as your freestyle, you can afford to take more strokes.

When you are ready to go from breaststroke to freestyle, one arm rows back to your thigh and you are swimming freestyle again. This can be also create a strong row and roll for air too if you need an extra breath of air. During the freestyle to breaststroke transitions and back, you can create additional opportunities for extra inhales and exhales. Placing your freestyle inhale right before your breaststroke tends to feel like you are getting an additional breath of air. And after your breaststroke, if you row and roll for air right away at full speed, it feels like you are getting another breath of air sooner than you normally would.

Chapter Nine – Sidestroke

The sidestroke is not just for life saving. As a lifeguard, you use the stroke to transport the "victim" back to land with a powerful scissor kick while one arm is kept locked around the victim so the victim doesn't panic and turn on you. Most of the propulsion comes from the kick. Like breaststroke, the arms serve mainly to direct your glide. Without a victim to pull, you may find this stroke to be a relatively easy stroke in terms of seeing, breathing and effort.

You can keep your head out of the water and consistently see while swimming the sidestroke. If you find breaststroke timing difficult, try the sidestroke where the timing is similar: gather, kick and glide while keeping your face out of the water. Depending on the difficulty that you are having with your other strokes, the sidestroke could be one of your fastest strokes during a triathlon because seeing allows you to stay on course. The downside though is that doing scissor kicks could tire your legs for the bike and run.

You continue to swim with a throw and row arm action during the sidestroke. The motion is like picking cherries in a tree with one hand and arm and then transferring the cherries to your other hand at the chest so they can be place in the bucket below your waist. When both hands are close to one another and at your chest, you throw and row simultaneously. Divide the work between the two arms so the throw helps your row.

Maintain a thumbs up technique with your throwing hand and arm. Your body is going to be on its side so your hand needs to be on its side too, with your palm facing the same direction as your face and body. Using a flat hand in the water to help position your body's weight is going to strain your shoulder's rotator cuff, therefore avoid a flat hand in the water. Position your weight between your upper chest and upper back, like you do when rolling for air in freestyle. Don't force your arms or legs to do the work that your chest and core could do for you.

Scissor kicks tend to be easier than breaststroke kicks. Scissors kicks are meant to be uneven with one leg above and the other below while coming together. The breaststroke kick on the other hand has the legs coming together at the same level. Therefore, it is hard to spot a poor scissor kick because the legs are meant to be uneven in the first place. A good scissor kick has knee bend, goes wide and with a powerful, straight legged scissor movement comes back together. Like the breaststroke kick it is useful to get away from someone else, too. As a lifeguard, the scissor kick allows you to quickly put some distance between you and a drowning "victim" that is trying to climb on top of you. In a triathlon for example, if someone was doing scissors kicks in front of you, it would be wise to swim around them rather than into their scissor kick. Their heel and not just their toes could hit you in the head which might really hurt.

Which leg is the top leg and which is the lower leg of the scissors is up to you. As a lifeguard, you had to be aware of not kicking the person you were bringing back to land so you adjusted your kick so as not to kick them. For the sake of speed and comfort though, you might find that one leg, left or right, is always better on the top or bottom regardless of how you are facing. Compare, contrast and play around with which leg is better closer to the surface and which leg is better lower in the water before you determine which combination to build upon.

A big benefit is the glide that you can maintain after the throw/row/kick combination. Like the breaststroke, you burn up excessive energy if you hurry the sidestroke. The sidestroke is better done at the tempo of a skating motion and rhythm. You compress your body. You jump. And, you glide in a long skating motion to complete one sidestroke.

In sidestroke, your core does a small crunch and then goes into a plank position for an effective glide. Engaging the core when you jump and holding it during the glide helps you build the core awareness and muscles that you want for backstroke and freestyle.

How much you position your weight on your side depends on you. The more that I am on my back positioning my weight on just one scapula or shoulder blade, the easier it is to swim sidestroke. I do remember being more on my side, when I was younger, when I had better flexibility. The amount that you are on your side depends on several factors so go through a series of exaggerated positions to determine what is wrong and what is right for you.

Develop your sidestroke on both sides. Conditions or the situation might not always allow you to stay on one side. You may also tire on your favorite side and want to switch to the other side for a break. For your health, you also want some symmetry to your body and swimming the sidestroke to your left and to your right will build symmetry and develop your core strength equally.

The side stroke does not have to be a slow stroke. Yet, for triathletes I suggest that you use it as an alternate resting stroke because it can tire the legs. Taking a few sidestrokes rather than breaststrokes or backstrokes is an option for those who can sidestroke better than the other resting strokes.

Chapter Ten – Butterfly

Swimmers do the butterfly stroke because some swimmers can and some of us can't. The butterfly is a stroke that requires a high level of skill, flexibility, timing and energy. Even children use a gradual and slow build up while developing their butterfly stroke.

For older swimmers just starting to swim and triathletes, I don't recommend doing much if any swimming with the butterfly stroke. You could try it for a few strokes. You could do it for twenty-five yards, maybe fifty yards, and then you would be spent. Investing your time in developing a butterfly stroke would probably be better spent on the other swim strokes, in my opinion.

Developing the dolphining core motion that is used to swim the butterfly is worthwhile. Your body moves through the water with an undulating, wave motion that begins at the chest and ends at your feet. Like the flutter kick, it is easier to do face down rather than on your back. Yet, once you can do the dolphin kick face down, you can challenge yourself to do the dolphin kick on your back to increase the effort, build your core and allow you to breathe.

My advice is to develop the dolphin kick that is the butterfly kick. You can try the shoulder and arm motion if you have the flexibility. You can try to put the timing together. And if you are successful, after all of that work, you will have a butterfly stroke that you would seldom use outside of training or an individual medley if you are an adult trying to learn the stroke later in life.

Chapter Eleven – Body mass influences your stroke

Momentum = Mass times Velocity

When my sons were swimming on the neighborhood swim team, it was pretty clear that the outcomes were being determined along the lines of mass. Because everyone was swimming in age groups, we were supposed to have children of approximately the same size competing against one another. When the boys and girls approached puberty though, you could have one hundred and fifty pound swimmers versus eighty pound swimmers. The outcomes of these races were pretty much decided by weight or mass. The one hundred and fifty pound swimmers, especially if they looked a little well rounded, were clobbering their smaller, skinny counterparts. Very few of the lighter swimmers could make up with stroke velocity and kicking what the heavier swimmers brought to the pool in terms of mass. Some swim strokes, like backstroke, were better than others for the lighter swimmers; yet on the whole, if everything else was equal, the lighter swimmers lost. We might as well have been watching the heavier and lighter swimmers wrestle on the pool deck to determine winners and losers.

Learn from my experience in choosing a stroke pattern that fits your size. While teaching many swim workshops, heavier swimmers would consistently outperform lighter swimmers. A heavier swimmer could take fewer strokes to cross the pool than a lighter swimmer. Some coaches attribute this to length or height and I attribute fewer strokes to mass or weight. Because there is a correlation to height and weight, I can understand how others came to their conclusion. Yet, I came to a different conclusion seeing short swimmers over 200 pounds perform as well as tall swimmers over 200 pounds.

Momentum is made up of mass and velocity. Mass is not height. Mass is weight. Your weight in the water is a positive because swimming is weight transfer. It is harder to keep something light moving on it's own, especially in a fluid as thick as water can feel at high speeds. Something that is heavy and moving resists inertia better and tends to keep moving on it's own. This too is momentum, the continued movement without further propulsion.

For example, the distance that it takes cars and trucks to stop without braking is a good comparison. Due to their momentum, it takes trucks much longer to stop because the trucks are heavier., more mass Due to their smaller mass, cars take much less time and distance to stop. You know from experience that a car can stop faster than a truck. Once trucks and cars are going at the same speed, trucks go farther, retaining speed better, when you lay off the gas and allow both cars and trucks to coast.

As this applies to swimming, every swimmer coasts even a little bit in between strokes. More massive swimmers do not slow as much in between strokes as compared to less massive swimmers. Physics favors massive objects. While small objects are making many, faster motions, don't be fooled by the benefit of action alone. Multiple motions are being employed to make up for a lack of mass. More motion is how smaller wrestlers or boxers or basketball players overcome a heavier opponent.

It puzzles some people that heavier triathletes consistently out swim lighter triathletes. It's also the exception to find a lighter swimmer out swimming the heavier swimmer. When I came across those few exceptions, it was obvious that the lighter swimmer had smoother skin, a better fluid dynamic body shape, and higher number of strokes and kicks to compensate for their lack of mass.

A good example of this is Total Immersion's Terry Laughlin. Terry's personal success is due to his weight and his technique. Many healthier, lighter swimmers using the same technique and swimming as hard as Terry do not get the same results that Terry does because they are simply lighter. Every swimmer would benefit from adapting a swim style that fits their weight, shape and skin rather than a swim style that does not fit them.

The physics are rather straightforward on this matter. If shape and skin surface are the same and without compensating by kicking, the 200 pound swimmer's ten strokes is equal to the momentum of the 100 pound swimmer's twenty strokes. If drag and shape are the same, and with no kicking, that is what it would take for both swimmers to cover the same distance at the same time. Look on the web for momentum calculators and you can try the numbers yourself.

A lighter swimmer needs more strokes and more kicking to offset their lack of mass. Lighter swimmers need to make up for their lack of mass with velocity. Lighter swimmers, normally, can more easily stroke more often and kick more often to offset the more rapid slow down that they experience in between strokes.

A heavier swimmer can make do with fewer strokes and less kicking due to their mass. Heavier swimmers may not want to speed up their strokes because they could lose some of momentum's economy of energy over a long swim by taking too many strokes.

There are many factors that influence movement through the water. The three biggest are your mass, shape and your skin. You can choose a stroke pattern that fits your mass or weight. You can reduce your skin's surface drag, somewhat. You can alter your shape, somewhat.

So while there are swim coaches that want you to speed up or slow down your stroke, solely based on their notion that more strokes are better or fewer strokes are better, you do need to do what is best for your shape, weight, skin and level of coordination. Take more strokes and kick more if you are light and you can stroke and kick less if you are heavy.

Another example is basketball. We often see what a mistake it is for the center to play basketball like a guard. The center doesn't have the laws of physics or a physique to play like a guard. And while the guard likes being quick, the guard can't do what the heavier center can do. And like basketball, most of the dominant swimmers today are like basketball's power forwards who can manage their weight optimally.

So if you were one of the many people who did not improve with the swim program that you tried. I hope this explanation of some of the physics involved in swimming helps you get back to a stroke count and rate that is optimal for your weight and coordination in the water.

When your momentum or speed in the water is already good, you don't want to slow your momentum by taking a swim stroke. Wait until you feel your momentum is about to slow before you take your next stroke. Movement for the sake of movement does not necessarily add to speed. While a goldfish benefits from moving it's body 100 times to cross a body of water, it would not benefit a whale to move it's body 100 times to cross that water. The whale could do it in one movement and trying to fit in ninety-nine more movements would not make it more effective.

Heavy swimmers especially need to make each stroke count and then reap the energy benefit of that stroke before they launch into the next stroke. In pool races of two hundred yards or less, which most pool races tend to be, this is harder to see; yet, in the longer swims, like triathlons and open water swims, this is easier to see and experience. If you are a heavy swimmer, it is hard to keep up a high stroke rate like a lighter swimmer can over long distances. If you are heavy, try slowing down your stroke to avoid breaking your already good momentum by stroking too early.

It takes patience with your swim stroke if you are a heavy swimmer. It is easy to jump to the wrong conclusion that a person needs to move to float (you don't) and that you need to keep up fast movements over a long distance. The heavier the swimmer, the more you need to learn to lay down a stroke and glide to reap the full benefit of transferring your "enormous" weight. Many people think that moving fast is swimming fast and this thinking is especially detrimental to you.

A heavy shot putter places his effort into one throw. A heavy swimmer would benefit from throwing his swim stroke forward like a shot putter stays in position for a moment after the throw. Those moments that you hold your weight steady in the water are moments where your momentum continues. Pulling out of that position before your momentum or speed drops is not beneficial to your long distance energy requirements.

The lighter the swimmer the need for more strokes.

If you are a light swimmer, be prepared to take more strokes. Your challenge is to make up for your lack of weight or mass with velocity. You need to be a sports car and not a truck. Your RPM needs to be higher, and it can be, to offset your lack of momentum in between swim strokes. You actually want to fit in more strokes in a pool length until you hit the point where more strokes does not add to your ease and speed.

A guard in basketball benefits from dribbling the ball for movement around the court. You will also benefit from taking more strokes than a heavier swimmer to get the same amount of work done. If someone was asking a 100 pound person to move a ton of weight made up of small pieces, the hundred pound person would benefit from doing it in more trips than a 200 pound person would want to take. A lighter person would then take their trips faster than the heavy person to accomplish the work in the same amount of time.

What is a good stroke count for a lighter swimmer? It is hard to say because your kick can help your momentum from slowing down. Kicking influences your stroke count. Consider that you could cross the pool with just one backstroke if you used your kick for the rest of your propulsion. However, that doesn't mean that it is best to take one arm stroke to cross the pool. If you are a light swimmer, add to your stroke count until you reach your optimal ease and speed.

Total Immersion coaches and other swim coaches use the approach of adding stroke count to the seconds it takes to cross a pool as a guide to optimal stroke count. While that may be an improvement over how you are currently measuring optimal stroke count, I am not completely convinced of that approach. Kicking can skew that result and too much kicking tends to hurt your results over long distances. Too much kicking also tends to be detrimental to triathletes who bike and run after their swim. Therefore I take the measurement of strokes and seconds over a short distance with some qualification.

In cycling and running, where you are also moving your weight with many of the same factors involved, your cadence in cycling or stride rate in running is what it is. On the bike, while you could use a bigger gear to increase the distance traveled with each pedal stroke your cadence or stroke rate and watts would tend to drop and not necessarily be more efficient. On the run, while you could increase your stride rate it would also be hard to keep or increase your stride distance. In cycling, running and swimming, we work either or both rate and distance to nudge up our speed.

As triathletes, think of the contrasts that we observe. A heavy cyclist in a thin medium like air finds that it is more effective to nudge up stroke distance. In running, where weight has to be lifted against gravity (unlike cycling and swimming), everyone's cadence is close to ninety strides per minute. We then see heavier runners excelling in the shorter races and lighter runners excelling in the longer races. For a light swimmer in a really dense medium like water, it is more effective to nudge up stroke count or velocity.

For your swimming, consider that you are moving your weight from here to there. Swim what it takes as far as stroke count to get there. Thinking that a reduced stroke count is more efficient is not always the case. The most efficient stroke count or stroke rate is the one that is easiest for you to sustain over a distance and not merely several pool lengths. It depends on your weight, shape and skin surface.

The smoother the body the need for fewer strokes.

A huge benefit that youth and most women have is a smoother body and skin surface. Compared to a fifty year old swimmer, children are Teflon coated. The smoother the skin surface, the more that drag is reduced and the greater the distance covered in between strokes, resulting in the need for fewer strokes. Light swimmers are often children or women and their smoothly superior skin surface adds to their speed in the water.

Like a cyclist buys a faster bike for increased speed without increased effort, a swimmer can increase their speed by buying materials (lotions and swimsuits) that smooth out their body's surface. You can buy lotions that are applied directly to the skin. For triathletes in the open water, a lotion like Bullfrog® sun block provides your skin with a really slick surface in the water. Later, on the bike and on the run, it reduces chafing too. However, in the pool, substances like Bullfrog can interfere with water quality if people use it. For open water races though, you can buy yourself some speed by using a high quality lotion that reduces surface drag.

In the pool and open water, swimmers can buy swimsuits with a surface smoother and faster than their own skin. The surface of these suits and the compression of the suits buys swimmers faster times. Swim federations have taken to regulating swimsuits so advantages created by technology don't determine race outcomes. Make certain that if you buy a bodysuit for swimming, that it does not exceed the rules in place.

Dry skin or a dry surface is also faster than a wet skin surface. That is why your first lap in the pool is often your fastest. The tiny air bubbles on your skin's surface can make your first length in the pool your fastest. It's a shame that those tiny air bubbles don't stay on us for the entire swim.

The rougher the body's surface the need for more strokes.

We hate to see wrinkles. Every wrinkle on the body creates a rougher surface and slows down a swimmer. Maybe we could develop swim masks for older swimmers to compensate for our wrinkles. It's not just wrinkles though.

Hair also slows a swimmer down. Again, children and women have an advantage with less hair and smoother hair than most men. Competitive swimmers and triathletes shave down to reduce the effect of hair, yet even the stubble at your skin level leaves a slower surface.

So if you are swimming next to someone whose skin surface is really smooth and yours is not, it is similar to their having smooth bicycle tires built for the road and you alongside them with nubby treaded bike tires.

The rounder the body the need for fewer strokes.

Who likes to be out-swum by fatter looking athletes? However, that is often the case. In addition to the advantages of weight and smoother skin surface, a rounder shape moves through the water better. We throw balls and spheres and not squares, triangles or rectangles.

Rounded is better than jagged and cut in the water. If you can see the ribs of someone swimming, the ribs are creating eddie waves and turbulence close to the body. As triathletes, we don't want to carry extra weight while running. We probably also like to see some muscle definition because it makes us look more "muscular",and healthy. However, looking more muscular creates more surface angles, more drag, and more turbulence. So while strength gains allow you to swim faster, muscle definition offsets some of the strength gain. Having finely defined muscles that you can see creates multiple surface angles that create more drag. So while someone who is really "cut", as they describe defined musculature, would appear to physically have an advantage, that is not the case. Swimming would be faster if muscles were covered by a layer of fat to create just one surface and not multiple surfaces underwater. As we know, boats, paddles and oars are smooth and single surfaced to reduce their drag in the water.

The swimmer with a rounder torso and upper body and narrow hips and legs has a better streamline and shape for swimming than a swimmer with a small upper body and large hips and legs. A cyclist whose legs have bulked up with a small upper body which has been worked less does not have a good shape for swimming. That cyclist might be in good "shape" yet the shape of their body is not conducive to swimming. People with small upper bodies who carry their weight in their hips and legs do not fare as well in the water.

Drag is proportional to the size of the wake that you leave behind you. Round shapes that gradually narrow down create less turbulence or wake in the water. A body shape that starts off narrow and then goes round creates more turbulence in the water.

Over time, if you stick with swimming, stretching and weight lifting your shape could change, somewhat. At one time I was a 130 pound cyclist and marathon runner and now I am a 155 pound triathlete. Most of the gain has been in the upper body due to the upper body demands that swimming has placed on me. Increasing the upper body not only provided more muscle to do the work, the bulk creates a better shape that creates less turbulence behind me.

If you are a triathlete and push a big gear creating big glutes and thighs, while neglecting your upper body, then you are working against creating the body shape that you would want for swimming. It would be better to spin more and run more to reduce your bottom half while on the other hand swimming and lifting weights to increase your upper body for the sake of swimming.

Tall, thinner swimmers tend to snake through the water.

Tall swimmers improve as they develop the knowledge and coordination to swim straight. Tall, lanky athletes have the advantage of long levers. In the world of physics, long levers are good if the levers are stable and controlled. What you often see though are tall people without the coordination to go with their height. Developing coordination is a key to your swimming and athletic success regardless of your size.

While tall swimmers have the potential to cover more distance with each stroke they also have the potential to go further inwards or outwards with each stroke. A long arm or a leg out of place and moving in less than a straight manner is much more noticeable with a tall athlete. The longer limbs are harder to control. Yet, once the tall athlete has developed strength and coordination at the joints and a body awareness, the levers work together better. When they optimally apply their levers, the tall athlete has physical advantages over the shorter athlete.

Sports are self-selecting. In gymnastics, a tall athlete has more trouble because smaller athletes can control their limbs (levers) more easily. In basketball, height is an advantage when there is sufficient limb strength and coordination to go with the height.

In a triathlon, you have three sports with differing physical requirements. In the water, it would be beneficial to be about two hundred pounds or more because your sheer mass helps propel you between strokes. On the bike, if the course is flat it would pay to be heavy and powerful. On the bike, if the course is hilly it would be better to be light and powerful. On the bike if you are light and lack power, the international triathlon races that allow you to draft on the bike is where you will find the most success. During the run, it pays to be light because you have to lift your weight against gravity. One of the challenges and satisfactions of the triathlon is that the sport does not favor one body size exclusively as gymnastics or running or swimming does.

Drafting is always allowed in open water swims and triathlons. I can't think of many good reasons not to draft behind your competition, especially if you are lighter than they are. Probably the only good reason not to draft is similar to the reason why some people don't draft while cycling, they don't have the coordination and ability to be just inches behind someone and are afraid to do so.

In cycling, riders vie for placement near the front of the pack so they can draft in a more favorable aerodynamic position. In a pack of cyclists the lead riders are battling the wind. Cyclists also avoid the rear of the pack for long periods. Because, while the rear of the pack is the most aerodynamic, the rear of the pack also carries the most risk. The risks in the pack are: someone in front of you slows or crashes causing you to lose contact with the pack; or you may have to expend more energy at crucial times to get to the front of the pack when everyone else wants to do the same. Cyclists often prefer to see the front rider without being the front rider until the finish line is in sight.

In swimming, even if you were the superior swimmer, it would be better to draft off the competition rather than have them draft off you and beat you in a sprint twenty-five yards from the finish of the swim. Perhaps you can share the work with the other swimmers for the best overall time results. However, if everyone is swimming for themselves, it will be the swimmer who feels compelled or confident to lead the others to the finish in front of the pack of swimmers.

Open water swimming could possibly be the swimming sport for lighter swimmers to get back into the sport and compete against the heavier swimmers. In cycling, the smaller sprinters are notorious for sitting on the wheel of heavier and stronger cyclists until the finish line is in sight. Then these sprinters, who are more nimble and faster over short distances, "jump" the other cyclists and pass them in a sprint at the end. Short course (25 meter pools) swim champions who do not have the same success in long course (50 meter pools) might consider drafting behind the heavier swimmers in open water races and then sprinting past their competition much like sprinters do in cycling.

In triathlons, it would make more sense to draft throughout the swim if you are focusing on your overall placement or time. If you want to be on record as the first out of the water, then you could sprint at the end and really annoy the swimmer that you were drafting off. You could also want to be just ahead of others leaving the water for the sake of having fewer people or nobody in front of you in the first transition. Having fewer people in the transition area has tactical and strategic benefits for the leaders as well as those in last place too

Over time, your upper body will increase to alter your shape.

If you are training correctly with more food and a proper diet, your body will gradually put on more muscle if your swim technique is correct. You do want to increase upper body weight for the sake of swimming. You also want to "push a bigger gear" or "skate" while swimming with your hands, arms, back and chest to develop more bulk.

If you continue "spinning with your arms" with a fast, yet inefficient stroke, you will build less muscle. Moving the arms fast without an effective row does not build muscle. An effective row builds upper body muscle. An effective row feels like your hand and arm are pushing against a solid surface rather than water.

A tall, lanky person could find it difficult to control their row because they might have to develop the coordination and strength at wrist, elbow and shoulder to create an effective row. Until you row properly, you really won't be building muscle mass and swimming effectively.

If you continue to kick your way through the swim, your kick could help for short distances, yet it could work against you for long distances.

Technique is important in all sports. Good technique gradually leads to a better body shape for the sport that you want to improve. The benefit of triathlon training is that you are improving more than one area of the body for your overall health.

Chapter Twelve -Core strength

Core strength helps spatial orientation.

Knowing where you are in the water is critical to your progress through the water. If you have body bend and body give, your head could be pointed in one direction with your body going in another direction. Though you can see, you don't seem to be going in the direction that you are seeing. Even in the pool with lane lines, you could be wandering from one side to the other.

You want core strength from your ribs to your groin to help your spatial orientation in the water. Your abdominal muscles are in four sections. The bottom section, below your umbilicus or belly button is especially important to your swim. You probably have the top three sections developed, more than the fourth, because you are visibly aware of them and because you use these three sections on land when bending down and up. The fourth and lowest section of abdominal muscles you dynamically engage when you are horizontal and lifting your legs up off of the floor. Because you are consistently working the vertical abdominal muscles on land and seldom lie down to work the horizontal abdominal muscles, you may not be aware of the weakness and unwanted give at your hips and waist.

All sections of the abdominal muscles must be engaged providing you with a strong platform and leverage for placing your weight high on your chest or back. If the lowest section is weak, then your strong chain of muscles is broken. The weak link is often the abdominal muscle below the belly button. When a chain's link is broken, it's hard to have a straight chain for straight swimming.

It's hard to be spatially oriented on a snaking platform. The more connected and engaged your body parts, the more successfully you know where you are at in the water and see where you are going. When you go swimming, notice how much better you sight at the beginning of your swim before your core tires.

Core strength creates a platform for your wheelbarrow and handles.

Core strength is critical to placing and keeping your weight on the front wheel of your wheelbarrow in the water. A wheelbarrow needs levers for leverage. If the levers were in several sections and one of the sections gave away, then it would be impossible to have the leverage to keep the weight high on the wheel.

You will visibly see in others and notice in yourself that your hips give and sink when you are on your back or roll up for air. You are not trusting the water to support your weight and you are not engaging the fourth section of your abdominal muscles to raise the hips and legs up in the water.

Face down in the water, you will visibly see in others or notice in yourself a deep kick in the water below the body. A problem with a deep kick is that it creates drag that offsets some of its propulsion. You also need horizontal lower back strength to lift your legs when you are face down.

Learning where the location of this core strength may be easier on land than in the water. Lie down on the floor with your back flat on the floor and lift and kick your legs. Due to the floor, your hips won't be able to give like they do in the water. Before long, with no water to help your legs float, you will notice your horizontal abdominal muscles tightening. That last section of abdominal muscles is critical to keeping your hips from sinking in the water. By rolling over face down on the floor, also continue kicking with your feet and legs off of the floor to notice the lower back muscles working that help keep you horizontal in the water.

Do five minutes of feet off the floor drill to develop your horizontal strength. For five minutes, while you are lying on your back, your side or your chest, keep your legs and feet off of the floor. Changing positions will help you accomplish five minutes and learn the various muscles involved in developing horizontal core strength. If you want to challenge yourself, stay with a position that you notice is a weakness for you. Your goal is to keep your legs off of the floor for five minutes straight. Doing this drill every other day will do a great deal for the core strength that you need for swimming.

Propulsion from the core can be powerful. Whether running or swimming, the power can come from the core and travel outwards through the limbs. While we often want to work our limbs for strength and speed, the origins of our movement comes from our core.

Walking comes from the hips, notably in between the hips and the lower back. When you can't call on those muscles and nerves to fire and work, it matters less how strong your legs and feet are. Muscle or flexibility imbalances in feet and legs can cause problems for your lower core. So, think of walking as a chain of events that begin with your lower core.

Swimming comes from the shoulders. The movement of the upper torso, back and chest, initiate the action that the arms follow. Think of swimming as a chain of events that begin with your upper core.

Two helpful swimming drills demonstrate the power of your core: the body dolphin and shoulder shrug.

The body dolphin movement is used in the butterfly and breaststroke. The core moves forward with a wave like motion. Dolphins move forward by moving up and then down and both core movement have them moving forward. The feeling or effect is that of a series of shallow dives in the water. From a chest up position, you move forward by going chest down. And, once the chest is down, you move forward again by going chest up. Your hips follow your chest in the rolling and waving action as your upper and lower core work together. The arms and legs are an extension of the core's movement, not the cause of it.

Likewise, shoulder, chest and back movements are used in freestyle and backstroke. The core moves forward with a walking like motion from the upper body. The reach forward in freestyle begins with your upper torso muscles. The action is similar to casting a line while fishing. While we see the fish line sailing through the air and the hand and arm in the chain of action, the casting action is much more powerful when we use the core and upper body. It's not like the fish line threw itself, or the hand threw itself or the arm threw itself, the chain of events began in the upper body.

To really swim well, you want your core involved and initiating the swimming movement. Throwing your core's weight into the movement makes swimming faster and easier than making just the arms or legs do the work. It's much better to launch your weight from your core and have the arms and legs react or follow.

Core strength maintains stability and maneuverability.

With every stroke, and a solid core, you could create the keel of a boat. The keel converts sideways motion into forward motion. Swim strokes, with an engaged core following, could become a series of mini-dives that propel you forward.

When you think about the faster marine animals a commonality is strong core. From vertebrae to vertebrae they don't have a break in the chain of muscle strength. This strength allows them to be highly stable and maneuverable at the same time. These animals are not content to relax and float. These animals are made to go.

How far can you go in developing core strength? Over time, you will go from awareness of core strength to complete control. You could go from lifting your feet off of the floor to upside down crunches hanging from your feet. Strengthen your core in a stretching manner from contraction to complete extension to gain the core strength in all four abdominal sections.

Chapter Thirteen– Flexibility

As good as Total Immersion is, they and others, were silent on how the lack of flexibility determines your swim stroke. When you have life long swimmers teaching adult beginners, the life long swimmers often don't understand that the life long swimmers have retained a flexibility that their students do not have. Flexibility determines body rotation, stroke entry, and kick.

With my approach to swimming, you are going to vary the movements to fit your current level of flexibility. If your neck is inflexible, you will roll side to side less. If your shoulder is inflexible, your stroke will enter the water sooner, at your shoulder. If your ankles and feet are inflexible, you will bend your knees more to compensate for a lack of toe point. As your flexibility changes, you can continue to custom fit your swim stroke by making changes to your technique. You will know the physics and reasons behind the actions so you can make conscious and positive changes to your stroke.

Neck

It is your neck that determines how much your body can roll from side to side. It frustrated me that Total Immersion would teach stacked hips and the FISH position. Adult students would come to workshops expecting to magically learn how to look over their shoulder in the water when they could not do so on land. Having read TI books and having seen the TI videos, they were under the impression that this was something that could be taught and was necessary for swimming. It took some understanding and demonstration on their part in front of a mirror to learn that their neck flexibility determined their body's roll.

The good news with neck flexibility is that it can improve and for the purposes of efficient swimming you just need forty-five degrees to the left and right to function well. The pendulum of a clock swings forty-five degrees to the left and then forty-five degrees to the right. Making the pendulum go to ninety degrees left and then ninety degrees right does not make the pendulum more efficient or change the time.

If you can't relax your neck to go forty-five degrees each way, begin working on your flexibility. Laying on the floor, with the weight of your head against the floor for resistance, let your eyes lead your look left and then look right. I prefer to do these movements slowly as the movement is as much about gaining relaxation while gaining some strength while stretching. You can also try ears to shoulders. You can look at the wall behind your head and then the wall at your feet. Keep the back of your head pressed against the floor for resistance, stability and guidance.

The tension that we carry in our necks hinders our swimming. Some people tend to drive themselves hard; yet, once they know that their performance depends on their ability to stretch and relax, they can learn to increase their neck flexibility.

Shoulders

Shoulder flexibility determines how soon the hand and arm enters the water. Flexible shoulders can extend the shoulder throw further forward which is advantageous. Inflexible shoulders stop sooner and create the need to have an earlier hand and arm entry into the water where you then extend the throw underwater.

There are definite benefits of extending the shoulder throw above water. First, it is easier and faster to move your hand and arm through air than water. Second, the weight of your body is thrown farther in front of you if you have the shoulder flexibility to do so. Third, shoulder flexibility range allows you to implement and feel more variety within your stroke. A flexible shoulder allows you to enter your stroke sooner or later in the water giving you a wider range to work in varying conditions.

Regardless of your range of shoulder flexibility, you want your throw to feel like you are delivering a punch or an eager handshake with your weight behind it. If you have the flexibility to throw or punch the water at a forty-five degree angle, go with that angle. If you have the flexibility to throw at a thirty degree angle, go with that angle. Swimming is weight transfer. You want to deliver your body's weight behind your throw or stroke. Regardless of shoulder flexibility the throw goes below your chest immediately to the "catch" or row position. When your throw goes directly to the row position, you have dropped your weight effectively in the water and you are in position to row without wasting any time or effort to move your hand into the "catch" or row position later.

From a standing position, and maybe in front of mirror, go degree by degree from directly punching over your head to punching at your chest or lower. Given your shoulder flexibility, some angle from your forehead to your chest will be the easiest and most forceful angle to throw your swim stroke with more of your body behind the throw. The force of the throw with the body's weight behind is more efficient and stronger than going for a long stroke above the water without the body's weight powering the stroke. Weight trumps length.

Feet and Ankles

Flexible feet and ankles help. Flexible feet and ankles create fins. Inflexible feet and ankles create picks. Picks are sharp, pointed instruments that pierce, indent, or dig into something. In the case of many adult swimmers, your feet could be more like picks than fins. After years of walking on land, it is hard to move your feet out of the ninety degree pick angle that the feet develop while walking and standing.

It's not easy to regain flexibility. You can make progress over time by stretching the feet and ankles in all directions. Do not make the mistake of overworking your toe point or you could develop a plantar fascia problem. Flexible feet and ankles will help you with your run and bike too, so it is worth the effort to make even modest gains with your ankles and feet. Besides stretching, foot massage can also help your feet.

You work with your lack of flexibility at the ankles and feet by bending your knees more while kicking in the water. Bending the knee allows the top of your foot to get horizontal rather than vertical to the surface. A horizontal foot acts as a fin, lifting and propelling. A vertical foot acts as a pick digging into the water slowing you down. The more inflexible the foot, the more your knee will have to bend. Keep bending your knee until you feel maximum water pressure on the metatarsals of your forefoot. You will get some lift from your thigh and foot pressing down during the kick by bending your knee. If you had flexible feet and ankles, your lower leg would also be pressing down with less knee bend for lift and propulsion. But, two out of three, foot and upper leg, is not bad. The trailing action that you do not want in the water is your feet creating turbulence at the tail end of your body with a picking action while you kick.

To make matters worse, people with inflexible feet incorrectly think they need to kick more rather than less. Because they think they can make up what they are missing with more kicking effort, they kick faster and harder. It's futile. Your lack of flexibility and the picking could actually have you going backwards while kicking. It would be better to go with the fewer kicks, or picks, if you have inflexible feet. I fall in this category and this is one of the reasons why I prefer a two beat kick, which is one kick per arm movement.

Joint

Joints are the focal points for your body levers. The more flexibility and strength that you have in your joints the greater the angle the joint can open and close. Wide angles with functional strength allow a person to maximize their size. Gymnasts tend to be small because their sport is all about creating wide angles with functional strength at the joints.

In swimming, you want to develop joint flexibility and functional strength. The most critical areas are your neck, shoulders, ankles, feet and elbows. Developing joint flexibility throughout the body will help your ability to swim. A lack of flexibility in one area makes you compensate in another area. The inflexible ankle and foot makes you compensate with more knee bend. The inflexible shoulder makes you compensate with an earlier hand entry into the water. An inflexible neck interferes with your ability to roll your torso from side to side to keep your weight constantly moving. And, a moving weight is easier to move than a stationary weight.

To develop joint flexibility, I recommend stretching with weights or stretching with resistance. Aim to create wide joint angles as you go through the motions of extension and contraction. Creating wider angles and wider functional strength creates more leverage. Being tall and having longer levers only helps if you also have joint flexibility and strength.

Like golf and other sports, your choices are to work with your lack of flexibility or gain more flexibility. Until you gain flexibility, work with what you have by compensating and swimming within your limits much like good golfers play golf.

Muscle

Muscle flexibility could be measured by the speed at which your muscle contracts and then relaxes rather than a range of motion. For example, children can have very loose muscles when resting and exercising. Their flexibility is demonstrated in going from contraction to relaxation quite rapidly. As adult athletes, it would pay to have muscles that are loosey-goosey like children. While range of motion is important as it helps us create more leverage, the ability to be able to quickly tighten and then relax the muscle is equally important.

We do, and can, swim, bike and run with muscles that remain somewhat contracted. However, it is much more efficient if the non working muscles relax. Are you flexible and relaxed or carrying tension through out your swim, bike and run? The flexibility to go from contraction to retraction (relaxation) is important. If opposing muscles remain somewhat contracted it takes more energy, your range of motion is restricted and speed slower when the opposing muscles remain somewhat contracted.

Resistance stretching helps your range of motion. To go further though, measure your ability to flip flop your muscles when at rest. Your calf muscle is a pretty good muscle to experience what I am suggesting. Can your calf muscle shake like jello or jelly when relaxed? Children can. You can too. A massage might help or laying in the sun for just ten minutes would help.

Once you can relax the muscle at rest, you can relax the muscles while moving. When the arm is moving through the air, out of the water, some of the muscles in the arm can be relaxed. There comes a moment of relaxation between these contractions or opposing muscles really are opposing one another.

In swimming and running, you can see a lack of muscle flexibility because the movements seem mechanical rather than flowing. Developing your flexibility to go from contraction to retraction develops a flow to your movement.

Awareness of the need to relax, during and after exercise, is another step in developing muscle flexibility. The more you train yourself to relax the more energy you will save. Otherwise, keeping your opposing muscles contracted is like running the air conditioning and heat at the same time. Pick any muscle group and work on going from contraction to relaxation. You might need to self massage the muscle. You might need to position the muscle to feel the times when it is more relaxed. You can teach yourself to have more muscle flexibility at rest and while moving. Start working on your ability to relax your muscles to save energy and gain speed.

Chapter Fourteen – Freestyle swim drills

Drills are important. Do drills more often than you "swim" if you want to change your swim stroke rapidly and dramatically. You will not be able to change your habits and muscle memory by just swimming. Your body returns to old habits and muscle memory if left to its own devices.

Musicians and golfers break down their "game" into separate actions. They don't presuppose that they can suddenly play a symphony or eighteen holes and be their best. They have drills and they practice the rudiments of their games to improve. Their drills repeat the new actions that they want to learn more frequently than playing a piece music or a round of golf would. They workout their flaws by doing repetitive drills that eliminate their tendency to play the music or the game the wrong way. Good musicians and golfers don't try to avoid their flaws to eliminate their flaws.

Swimming drills of all kinds existed before today's coaches were born. Every drill that I am explaining to you may have existed in one form or fashion before me. It is the reason and understanding for the drill that could be different from what others have offered to you in the past. Hopefully, I am explaining the art of swimming better than you have heard it in the past. Swimming been described for quite a long time. God, the first coach, talks about swimming in Isaiah 25:11: "And he shall spread forth his hands in the middle of them, as he that swims spreads forth his hands to swim". So God, speaking through Isaiah tells us that swim technique involves putting forth your hands and arms to swim. This may be first written description of swimming and today we still have a multitude of coaches trying to describe swimming.

THE FIVE BASE DRILLS ARE WHEELBARROW, HANDLE, BACKSTROKE, UNDERWATER SWIMMING, AND SHOULDER STROKES.

Freestyle kicking drills: wheelbarrow, handle, backstroke.

You won't be needing a kick board or fins with these kicking drills. You want your drills to replicate to real swimming positions in the water. While kick boards let you keep your head out of the water, you actually want to practice kicking with your head in the water. Fins hide or mask the problems with your kick and you actually want to drill like you swim.

ONE -The wheelbarrow kicking drill

The wheelbarrow drill has you kicking with your hands on your front thighs and elbows in your ribs. Your hands and elbows stay there. You can begin either face down in the water or face up on your back. In many ways, this simple drill without the use of your hands and arms is the most difficult drill of all. Be patient with yourself. Move onto other drills and come back to this drill over your lifetime.

Throughout the wheelbarrow drill, both hands and arms are positioned with your hands on your front thigh and your elbows in your ribs. You don't take a stroke during this drill. You want hands and arms tight into the body creating positive tension. You do want to have an awareness that placement of your hand, elbow or arm behind your spine does not work as well. They inhibit your rolling action when they are behind your spine. If you get sloppy, your arms can become like tree limbs protruding from a tree inhibiting the tree to roll in the water. It is better to keep your hands and arms close and tight to your body to help you streamline your roll for air. The hand on your thigh that is higher in the water is also useful as a gauge to let you know that your hips are up and level. If that hand on your thigh is not breaking the surface of the water, then you have weight at your hips below the water level and not on your chest or back which is the the front of your "wheelbarrow".

The wheelbarrow drill is named the wheelbarrow because the concept is that it is a challenge to position your weight on just one "wheel", your chest. Like a wheelbarrow, it's initially hard to get the weight of the wheelbarrow over the wheel in order to move the weight. Once you do get the weight positioned over the wheel of the wheelbarrow, it becomes much easier to move the weight. Most people want to position their weight at their hips because that is what we do on land. You really have to work at moving the weight from your hips to your chest/back. When you notice yourself sinking in the water, you will notice that your weight shifted to your hips.

Balancing your weight at your chest/back and not your hips is one of the tricks to swimming. Some swimmers have learned to do it naturally and unconsciously. If you look at successful swimmers, they have their chests as low as their hips and are much more level than non-swimmers. A goal of the wheelbarrow drill is to get your weight positioned in the water. Some people are more comfortable beginning on their backs with their face out of the water. Some people are more comfortable beginning face down in the water. Either way you start, you learn to roll up or down. Until you learn how to roll up, you can stand up in the pool while beginning to learn the wheelbarrow. I would rather you stand instead of cursing me and this drill. This drill is not to be used for water boarding prisoners.

On your back, you want to position your weight on one scapula or shoulder blade. Face down in the water, you want to position your weight on either your left chest or the right chest. Don't aim to position your weight on both scapula or both pectoral muscles at the same time. We won't be swimming flat on our backs or flat on our chests so we won't be drilling flat. You will roll from left scapula to left pectoral muscle and back to left scapula. After you practice the left side of your body, you will practice the right side of your body by going from right scapula to right pectoral muscle and back to your right scapula. This is the direction you roll when swimming and it is the direction you roll while drilling. You roll up 90° and then you roll down 90° to breathe on the same side while swimming. Don't do 360° rolls to breathe while drilling.

Exhaling out your nose underwater is fundamental to this drill and swimming. Exhaling out your nose prevents water from going up your nose. Some people learn to exhale out their nose underwater by simply placing their head underwater and timing how long they can continue to exhale. At first, a person might exhale in a second or less and eventually develop an exhale that last for ten seconds or more. While not getting water up your nose is the immediate and urgent goal of exhaling from your nose, the main benefits of exhaling underwater is getting rid of the carbon dioxide in your blood stream and not having to share the time, when you want to inhale, with an exhale and inhale. Expect to work on your exhale as long as you swim. Every time you go for a swim, establish your exhale and your breathing pattern first before thinking about your technique. Only after you have your need for air taken care of will you be able to think clearly.

Developing your kick is not an easy task because we feel our legs underneath and behind us on land. In the water, you want to feel as if your legs and feet are movin in front of you. Many triathletes who come from a running or cycling background continue to move their legs like they are running or cycling in the water. Kick drills will change your runner's or cyclist's kick to a swimmer's kick. The backwards motion of the legs is counterproductive because it actually catches water and moves water in the wrong direction. Some runners and cyclists can see that they go nowhere or even backwards when they kick in the water in this way.

The forward kick is like kicking or juggling a ball in front of you. You want to hurry and keep your kick forward, not backwards. It's important to keep the action or the force forward and reduce backwards force. You want to feel water pressure on the front of your foot and leg.

Many coaches encourage their swimmers to have a straighter leg while kicking forward. Yet, you want to modify that straight leg with some knee bend to allow the foot to feel more water pressure on the front of the foot. Many runners, cyclists and walkers have inflexible feet due to years of land based activity. It is hard for them to point their toes. In the water, your feet may look like they are still walking or running even though you are trying to point your feet. If your feet are in the same position in the water that they are in land, then you won't feel much water pressure on the front of your foot. While using fins would temporarily mask the problem, they won't correct the problem. To adjust or modify your kick forward so you can feel more water pressure on the forefoot, bend your knees if needed. Bend your knees enough while kicking to feel water on the front of your foot.

Your roll to the side, not lift to the side, is a challenge. It is relatively easy to roll down in the water because it is less of a challenge to your inner ear and spatial orientation. However, rolling up for air for the new swimmer is more of a challenge as ear, eyes and abdominal muscles work in unison; or, your weight will go to your hips. We are all relatively inexperienced when it comes to going from face down in the water to face up. When doing the wheelbarrow drill, I encourage swimmers to frequently practice the roll up for air and not overdo staying in the easier face down position.

Remember that the entire roll only covers ninety degrees. The ninety degrees is made of two forty-five degree angles. One is face down with your body at a forty-five degree angle The other is face up with your body at a forty-five degree angle. Your head turning straight up or straight down, while your kick, completes the rotation. You may find it much easier to roll on your left rather than roll on your right side. Remind yourself to exhale to avoid getting water up your nose when you roll up. Continue to kick throughout your roll up. Avoid making 360° rotations or circles. Roll up and down on the same side. To work both sides of your body, pick a wall and roll towards that same wall when drilling back and forth in the pool.

Many people want to spend most of the time face down kicking because it is comfortable. What they really need is to practice the roll up more often while building their kick upwards and forwards on their back. Kicking upwards against gravity will develop your kick faster and better than kicking face down. The kicking resistance upward is greater and you have to engage your lowest abdominal muscles to a greater extent. Do not shorten the time you spend on your back during kicking drills or your reduce the effectiveness of the drills. Four to eight seconds face down and four to eight seconds face up on your back would be a good mix.

A good land based drill to develop a forward kick is to be on your back either on a bed or the floor and kick forwards and upwards for several minutes to learn a forward kick and to engage your lower abdominal muscles. At the pool, lie on the pool deck and kick over the water without your heels touching the water.

Neck flexibility determines the angle you will be on your side while swimming. You do want to roll from left to right and back while swimming. Yet if your neck is stiff and inflexible, you will not roll easily and an inflexible neck tends to make you flat in the water when face down and on your back. To gauge how flexible your neck is look in a mirror and move or roll your shoulders and body and not your head. How far you can roll your body left or right without your face moving an iota is a good gauge of neck flexibility.

If the wheelbarrow drill feels difficult when you are on your side, you could be on your side too much, beyond the flexibility of your neck. A flexible neck is good because it determines the range of side to side roll and ease of roll. Don't be preoccupied if you can not roll all the way left or right for a total of of 180°. Grandfather clocks work just fine swinging 45° degrees to the left and then to the right for a total of 90°. Likewise, if your neck flexibility can go 45° degrees to the left and right for a total of 90°, then you have enough flexibility to swim efficiently. Regardless of your neck flexibility, when you go beyond your neck flexibility you experience more difficulty and your hips sink.

Abdominal muscles, especially the lowest set of abdominal muscles and obliques, need to be engaged or somewhat contracted. Because of our land based experience we expect bend at the waist. In water, bend at the waist begins a sinking motion that forces you to kick harder to continue swimming. The more that you engage the abdominal muscles and obliques, the less you sink at the waist. Fish don't have waists, as we think of the waist. And, if we get rid of our waists in the water, we will swim much better.

For freestyle and backstroke, it would help if your core abdominal muscles were like a board or a pole with little to no give. I like to think of the Pilates "plank" position while swimming freestyle or backstroke. I also have a mental image of how well a plank of wood can be pushed from a dock and glide through the water. For the purpose of rolling to air, you want to roll without bending or sinking at your waist. I like to think of a log, without branches, rolling in the water as it goes down river. The momentum of the log keeps it rolling with little effort on the log's part.

For the purpose of kicking less, you want to reduce compensating kicking in order to level off. You want to kick for propulsion rather than leveling. Whenever, I have to kick out of a situation with either a lot of little kicks or a big compensating scissor kick, I know that my hips gave and sank and now I have to direct my energy to getting my weight correctly positioned to stop sinking.

If you know how to use a pull buoy, notice how the buoy helps prevent the give at the waist and has you rolling like a log without a kick. Many distance swimmers are faster swimmers with the pull buoy rather than kicking. This supports the idea that kicking is rather inefficient and not a good return on oxygen. If you are swimming a short distance, kicking helps lower your time. If you are swimming a long distance, kicking is not as efficient a means of propulsion as using your arms and might increase your time. Engage your abdominal and oblique muscles to create the pull buoy effect to reduce your kicking. Kicking drills, that correctly position your weight, could be the end of having to kick hard to swim.

TWO - The handle kicking drill.

Whatever you want your body to do in the water, having your hand and arm do it first makes your swimming easier. The "handle" is your extended hand and arm. The handle adds an extension to the wheelbarrow. The handle kicking drill is easier than the wheelbarrow drill. Your extended hand and arm create positive tension in front of your shoulder and set the tone for your entire body. Your handle can also initiate upwards and downwards rolls while helping your to position your weight on your chest and scapula.

Think of this drill as going from a backstroke position to a freestyle position and returning to the backstroke position, without taking a stroke, only kicking. Your arm remains extended straight in front of your shoulder, not your head. More accurately, in front of your shoulder extending comfortably to a place below your chest when face down in the water.

Your other hand and arm is positioned with your hand on your front thigh and your elbow in your ribs. You want the hand and arm, on thigh and rib, tight on your body creating positive tension too. Remember from the wheelbarrow kicking drill to create an awareness that your hand, elbow and arm behind your spine does not function well. Again, if you get sloppy with your arms you become like a tree with tree limbs protruding from the tree inhibiting the tree to roll in the water. It is better to keep the hand and arm that are not leading you close and tight to your body to help you streamline and not hinder your roll. The hand on your front thigh is also useful as a gauge to let you know that your hips are up and level. If that hand on your thigh is not out of the water, then you have weight at your hips and they are sinking resulting in having to kick harder to overcome the sinking hips.

How does your handle help you? Your extended hand and arm helps you position your weight on your scapula and pectoral muscle on that same side of your body. If your left arm is extended, your weight will be on your left scapula face up or left pectoral muscle face down as you kick. The extension of your arm creates some leverage where there was no leverage before. The helpful difference that the leverage makes in positioning weight can be compared to positioning weight with a wheelbarrow versus positioning weight with a teeter totter. It is much easier to position a teeter totter than a wheelbarrow due to an extension over the pivot point or fulcrum.

Your extended hand and arm helps you lead your body. Dancers and ice skaters have demonstrated that if you want the body to do something have the hand and arm lead the movement. Ballet consistently uses hand and arm movement to lead the body. In a fluid environment, like water, this is especially true. It's hard for your body to roll in one direction if your hands and arms are staying behind. Don't have your body and arm going in the opposite directions.

When you want to roll up for air, have your hand and arm in front of you initiate the lead and roll. Do not keep your hand and arm flat or thumbs down or they hinder and cut short the roll for air. Hold onto a desk in front of you, as an example, and roll away from your flat hand as if trying to breathe. If you notice your shoulder or rotator cuff tighten, your body will want to end the feeling of impingement by having your hand and arm come to your side. Notice how much longer your swim strokes are except for that stroke when you roll for air. The normal, yet incorrect, stroke pattern for many swimmers is long, long, short. Usually you feel two quality strokes before an inferior shorter stroke when rolling for air. This drill is designed to help you learn to have your hand lead your body so that all of your strokes are longer and of a high quality, especially when you roll up for air

During the handle drill, you want your abdominal muscles engaged like a plank. Extending the arm, as if you are reaching, pulls and engages the abdominal muscles and reduces your hip give. On land, reaching for the top shelf helps you to experience how extending your hand and arm engages core strength and helps you get what you want. Bending your elbow though reduces the positive tension that you had. Your hand and arm represent your body in the water. Your hand is your head. Your wrist is your neck. Your forearm your torso. Your elbow your waist. And, your upper arm your legs. If you get your hands and arms right, your body will be right. If you get your hands and arms wrong, your body will be wrong.

The first time you try the handle kicking drill, you might want to stay on your back or stay face down for awhile. Stand up for air, if needed. On your back, stay in a backstroke position without taking a stroke and only kicking for propulsion. Face down, stay in a freestyle position with your hand in the ready to catch or row position below your chest without taking a stroke and only kicking for propulsion. Exhale underwater, angle your body at forty-five degrees and kick with a forward kick as you did in the wheelbarrow drill. Stand up when you need air. The only difference so far is that you added a lever to help you position your weight on one side more easily. You are not flat on your back or chest when doing this kicking drill.

You do want the palm of your hand to be in agreement with your body. When you are flat in the water, your hand can be flat in the water. When you are on your side swimming at a 45° angle, you want your hand to also be at 45°. When you want to roll up for air at 90° or more, you want your hand and arm in front of you to be at the same angle, leading the way. Keeping the palm and body in agreement also has the hand, arm and body working together in the same direction.

Keeping the palm and body in agreement is shoulder neutral and helps prevent a common swimming injury, the rotator cuff. The old thumbs down technique has been debunked for a while, yet the technique is still out there. The problem with thumbs down is that it puts the hand and arm at odds with the body and you feel impingement in the shoulder or rotator cuff.

A thumbs down entry, catch and pull was popular because it was thought to give a better catch and rowing action. Yet you can catch and row in several ways that are more advantageous to your flexibility and functional strength. In other words, your catch or row can be customized to meet your physical characteristics too. Asking you to swim exactly like someone else only works well if you are exactly like the other person. Take the reasons behind my advice and apply them to yourself to customize your swim stroke to swim your optimal stroke.

The next progression in the handle (hand and arm) kicking drill is to use your handle to initiate the roll up or down. Whether you are on your back or face down, you want your hand and arm leading the way and in agreement with your body angle which is means a thumb up (or your pinky down) hand position throughout.

You will find it easier to train ten percent of your body, your hand and arm, than to train the remaining ninety percent of your body. While it may seem hard, if you can't get your hand and arm under control, then how much harder would it be to get your entire body under control. In the past, your body rolled and the hand and arm did not which had you wondering why rolling for air was so much harder than just swimming head down without inhaling. What does work better, is now you have your hand and arm and the body in agreement, doing the same motion.

The result of the dysfunction of not having the hand and the arm in agreement with the body is that the shoulder protects itself by having the hand catch and pull or row to early. So instead of allowing you time to inhale, the premature catch and pull (row) sinks the body, at the moment the hand and arm sink, cutting off the inhale. Instead of gliding and inhaling with an arm in front of you, your arm sank to bottom and then you sank with it before you were finished inhaling. This is not a huge error for swimmers in sprint events because they seldom breathe, if at all. The only damage would be to their shoulders while the performance damage would be minimal. Yet, for a distance swimmer relying on good inhales, the error is cumulative and takes away from your performance.

The handle kicking drill teaches you that you can maintain an arm in front of you while rolling up for air and while rolling back down. You learn that a longer glide for visibility and an inhale is doable. You learn to use your hand and arm as a lever to better position ninety percent of your body's weight. You learn the correct holding or catch position for freestyle and backstroke. You protect your head at all times with a fully extended hand and arm in front of your shoulder. You learn that extending the hand and arm engages the abdominal muscles and hips creating positive tension that streamlines and positions you in the water. You learn that the hand and arm lead body movement.

THREE The backstroke kicking drill.

The third kicking drill is the backstroke kicking drill. I want you to emphasize the kicking and downplay the number of strokes you take. In twenty-five yards, you might take four to six strokes. Normally, people like to row, row, row. In this kicking drill, you keep your core engaged and your kick going. You only reward yourself with a stroke when your weight is correctly positioned. You move your weight from the left scapula to the right scapula when you throw then row. Be at forty five degrees on your left side while your left hand and arm is leading and forty five degrees on your right side when your right hand and arm is in the water. Don't be flat on your back and don't let your weight go to your hips when you take a stroke. You limit your strokes because you are training yourself a new stroke timing, throw before you row.

Your face is directly straight up while doing the backstroke kicking drill. Your body rolls from left to right about ninety degrees in the water without your head rolling. Again, the exact amount that you roll from side to side is based on your neck flexibility. When you go beyond your neck's flexibility, you strain your neck and your hips begin to sink. You might find that it helps to look at lines on the ceiling if you are indoors to help your head remain straight up, so you can better feel the body roll while swimming straight.

Kicking on your back develops the forward kick that you want as a swimmer. If you have a running or cycling leg motion while doing backstroke, then your legs fall behind and below you. Your legs catch the water hindering your progress when you kick behind your body. Kick up and forward as if your goal is to get your toes and legs out of the water. Again, its easier, and wrong, to kick behind your hips, back and down. It's much harder to kick up and forward which makes this an excellent drill to develop your kick.

The backstroke drill has you kicking against gravity which means more resistance than you would find kicking face down. The backstroke drill allows you to work on your kick while breathing is less of an issue because you are face up. Because you are on your back a hundred percent of the time, you keep your core engaged and hips up a hundred percent of the time. The hand on your thigh is feedback that you are level as in the other kicking drills.

Limit your strokes. Taking too many strokes takes away from the core workout and kicking that you want to accomplish. Limiting yourself to a few strokes helps you really work the obliques well before taking a stroke which then works your obliques on the other side of your abdomen.

The backstroke drill is an important drill to start the development your stroke timing. Your new stroke timing is a throw before row rhythm. A row, row, row rhythm basically has one arm at a time doing the work. A throw before you row rhythm has two arms doing the work together. One arm moving forward over head (throwing) with the one arm moving backwards in the water (rowing) is twice as effective as just one arm at a time rowing. Two hands and arms working together are better than one.

Imagine that you want to tear something thick in half. If you use two hands, it's twice as easy. Imagine that you want to jump up to get a can of peaches off a high shelf. You can try to get the peaches by pushing down on a lower shelf. You can try to get it by jumping and reaching. Or you can try to get it by using a combination of jumping and reaching while pushing down on the lower shelf. That effective combination of jumping and reaching and then pushing down is the concept behind "throw before you row". When you throw before you row, you can teach yourself to break the single arm, one arm after the other, swimming that you were doing with row, row, row.

Initiate the action that you want by beginning with the easiest movement

An important concept of physical activity that I want you to learn is to initiate the action that you want by beginning with the easiest movement.

Moving your arm through the air is easier than moving your arm through the water. There is less resistance in the air. Therefore, if you want to go faster, begin by speeding up the movement that occurs in the air. While swimming, it is easier to speed up (or just maintain a speed) by moving the hand and arm through the air a little faster. It is easier to throw through the air rather than row the water. The throw is the easier movement and it can help to overcome the inertia of the row in the water if your technique is correct.

High jumpers use the concept of throwing their hands and arms over the high jump bar before their hips and legs effectively. High jumpers used to jump over the high jump bar with a land based orientation. Then Dick Fosbury introduced a new technique that involved throwing the hand and arm to lead the body's roll over the high bar. Today, almost every high jumper is using Fosbury's technique where the hands lead the body. I want you to think of that technique while swimming. Throw before you row.

If you have been rowing all of your life, it will take some focus to throw first. You might have so much rowing muscle memory that it will take concentration to keep one arm in front of you while you throw the hand that is on your thigh before you row with the hand in the water. More students have had success focusing on keeping the rowing hand in front rather than focusing on the throwing hand coming forward.

In the backstroke drill, you are not limited on air time so you do have the time to think about what you are doing without running out of air. You would be better off doing just four "throw before you row" strokes because your old habit was probably twenty rows. Speeding up will get you back to your old habits faster than into your new habits. Since you can breathe with your face up, take your time to feel the hand and arm leave the thigh in a straight armed throwing motion over your shoulder before the hand in the water rows.

The hand in the water does not stay where it is until the throwing hand reaches the water. As soon as the throwing hand is above the hip or chest, it is fine to row with the hand in the water. The greater your flexibility, the longer you can wait to row. The less your flexibility, the sooner you will want to row to take any strain off your shoulder.

The backstroke kicking drill also improves your shoulder flexibility and helps you learn how to bring your shoulders back into a good posture. Too often we spend most of the day with shoulders forward at the desk, while driving, and while swimming face down. On your back, you have the opportunity to work the shoulders back by throwing before you row.

Rowing shortens and tightens the muscles in your back, whether you are face down in the water or face up on your back. The backstroke kicking drill provides an effective stretch for the back muscles when you throw before you row. Your throw can completely stretch and lengthen the muscles and vertebrae. After a run, you might especially enjoy a cool down swim that restores your height with some throws before you row during backstroke.

FOUR - Underwater swimming drill.

When I went to New York, to be trained as a Total Immersion instructor by Terry Laughlin, Terry brought us a huge fellow that Terry had earlier used in his videos as an example of how not to swim. I felt sorry for this fellow as I thought someone by now would have taught him to swim in exchange for being in the video. This huge man swam about as well as Frankenstein walked.

I used the underwater swimming drill that day to help this huge fellow and get him swimming. He and I were thrilled that he finally had some coordination and a sense of swimming. My reasoning behind using the underwater swimming was that his huge mass was too much for anyone to guide as Total Immersion recommends. However, he could move his own mass by moving his hands and arms underwater to swim. As I look back, this was one of my earlier experiences as a coach that led me to realize the importance of mass, flexibility, and coordinating your mass rather than swimming long and tall in the water. This represents a divergence from Total Immersion or a new starting point in reasoning because my conclusions then followed based on moving mass rather than creating length in the water.

The underwater swimming drill starts out simply by taking two, three or four underwater strokes and then rolling up for air into the handle kicking drill (or backstroke) position. Your hands and arms stay underwater. Perhaps your elbows sneak up and out of the water, yet the strokes are largely underwater.

The primary concept that you want to learn in the underwater swimming drill is that your weight transfers more effectively (easily and powerfully) in front of your body. It is easier and more effective for your weight to roll from the left to the right and back to the left with outstretched arms in front of you.

Before you get in the water, extend both arms in front of you and roll your body back and forth by simply rolling your extended arms back and forth. Using a mirror to see your shoulders move in unison and your body roll side to side with your arms may help you. In the water, you transfer your weight more easily from side to side and forward by taking your throw before your row in front of you.

As you do on land, you transfer more weight by taking a bigger stride forward when walking or running. If you pushed off with your foot, neglecting the stride forward on land, you would be transferring your weight less effectively. With either walking or running you can more easily lengthen your stride by moving the leg through the air before your other foot leaves the ground with a push off. The foot and leg in the air has the effect of giving you an impressive push off as a consequence of the movement in the air. The leg through the air did most of the work; yet, the leg on the ground gets most of the credit to the casual observer. In running, we kick our leg forward before we push off. In swimming, throw before you row.

The purpose for not taking your arms or stroke out of the water in this drill is that I don't want to address your shoulder flexibility yet. Some people have shoulder injuries or very inflexible shoulders. The underwater swimming drill does not require flexible shoulders. The hands and arms stay in the water underneath you when taking your strokes. In the underwater swimming drill, you want to feel like you are crawling through the water.

"The crawl" was another name for freestyle at one time. I like the concept of calling it the crawl because a baby who just rows, rows, rows has a tendency to fall on its face. Once the baby learns to extend its arm, or throw it forward, the baby's crawling becomes easier, more stable, faster and effective.

The underwater swimming drill can teach the "throw before you row". You keep one hand in front while you bring the hand that was on your thigh forward. When the forward moving hand is parallel to the wrist or forearm that is in front, then you can row taking the front hand back to the thigh. Before you row, or catch and pull, you

117

want your throw to be propelling you forward. The arm coming forward will help create an effective momentum which makes your row look great. You want your throwing hand to reach and extend beyond where your rowing hand and arm were.

In walking and running we do more than move the back leg up to the foot that is on the ground. In walking and running we know that it is important to extend or kick the leg further forward. A problem with just pushing off in walking (or rowing in the water) is that you are some mass backwards in order to go forwards. You are not getting a 100% return on your investment in effort when you send some mass backwards in order to send some mass forward.

Weight transfer with the underwater swimming drill works well for all swimmers and especially well for large or uncoordinated or inflexible swimmers.

When you do the underwater swimming drill remember to: see, exhale underwater, have your weight on your chest, put forth your hands and arms to swim (throw before you row), focus on your weight shifting in front of you with your extended arm staying in place, until the arm moving forward gets to the extended arm's wrist, and then row. After you do two, three or four underwater strokes and before you run out of air, roll to your backstroke position to inhale. Even in this drill spend about fifty percent of your time face down and fifty percent face up to take the time to do it right.

Do not hurry your underwater strokes and exhale like you are swimming. When people hurry their strokes, they tend to row first. The trick is breaking the row first habit. It really takes a great deal of concentration on the part of many people to keep the front arm extended. Too many people jerk back the row and then extend the throw.

Go slow when you start with your underwater swimming. The goal is not to go fast during this drill. Your goal is to find that point where, with both hands in front of you, your weights tips from one side to the other and you begin experiencing seemingly effortless swimming propelled by shifting your weight in front of you rather than under you. Find your tipping point in front of you. Crawl like a baby underwater and you will learn like a baby that it is the forward moving arm that leads you.

FIVE - Shoulder strokes drill

The fifth drill of my five base drills is the shoulder stroke drill. The base drills are the wheelbarrow, handle, backstroke, underwater swimming and shoulder stroke. There are more drills, yet I recommend you become proficient at the base drills that break your bad habits first.

The shoulder stroke drill has you taking your arm out of the water like you are swimming. The big difference is that you put your stroke right back in the water at your shoulder. Your focus is not to extend your arm forward beyond your head. Your focus is to drop your arm and your weight into the water at your shoulder and then underwater to full arm extension. Regardless of one's flexibility, you feel like your stroke is entering the water parallel to your shoulder and not your head.

Most people react to swimming by reaching over the water. While I like the idea of moving the arm through the air, I value the idea of dropping your weight into the water as an even easier movement that will propel you. On land, extend and move your hands directly above your head towards the sky like you are swimming. You will probably feel that moving your hands directly above your head, even while you are out of the water, is rather awkward. Now, extend and move your hands at shoulder level. At shoulder entry, you will find more comfort and power. You want to throw your stroke into the water at your shoulder to maximize comfort, power, and an effective dropping of your weight. You then extend your reach to a full extension in the water.

With the shoulder stroke drill, your arm has just dove into the water rather than belly smacking into the water. Compare your throw to a belly smack, where you reach far in the air and then land flat on your forearm, versus a nice smooth dive, where you quickly get your forearm under the water's surface. You want you to get your arm into the water at your shoulder so your stroke is not belly smacking in the water in front of you.

Exaggerate the shoulder stroke drill so it feels like a deep dive that goes to the catch or row position. In normal swimming, you will not exaggerate the dive. However, if you don't find "the exaggeration" in drill, you probably won't find the difference between too much and too little of a dive. A good angle for your arm after it enters or dives into the water is an angle of 45° or half way between straight down and the surface of the water during this drill

Shoulder flexibility does affect your shoulder stroke. This then affects when you put your hand and arm in the water. It is the least flexible among us that need to put their arms in the water sooner. I have worked with swimmers whose shoulders were so inflexible that these swimmers swam better with underwater swimming rather than taking their arms out of the water. This is not any different than it is on land where people with little flexibility in their hips have to shuffle and put their feet on the ground sooner.

Swimmers that have very flexible shoulders can extend their arms and shoulder and drop their weight further in front of their shoulder. The difference at the shoulder between a flexible shoulder and an inflexible shoulder is only several inches at the shoulder. Yet, several inches at that pivot point makes a huge difference in dropping your weight forward more effectively. And, this is similar to walking or running where flexible hips help walkers and runners move their legs and their weight forward more easily without chopping their strides.

When doing this drill, you want to feel how far forward your shoulder can come with your hand in the water, upper arm perpendicular to your body, elbow as far away from your body as possible, and forearm dangling straight down. DO NOT point your hand or forearm inwards towards your head or body at any point in the motion forward.

On land, you want to look like a scarecrow with your upper arm to your elbow straight out to the side, yet the forearm hanging straight down. Because to really drop or throw your weight effectively, your body is going to follow behind the forearm. Many people get it wrong by throwing or taking their stroke to the center or their body in front of their head. Try to do work directly with your hands and forearms over your head, like many people swim, and notice how inefficient and awkward it is. Many swimmers tend to bend the forearm towards their head. They do so because of several mistaken beliefs. The two most prominent mistakes they make in their thinking is that it is more streamlined to swim with your hands in front of your head (it is not, it is just a weaker point to drop and leverage your weight from while swimming) and they tend to row, row, row.

Your upper arm and elbow come up out of the water away from your shoulder. I like the fingers to maintain contact with the water, because if the fingers and hand start reaching over the water, I want you to feel the loss of contact with the water. Rather than taking a stroke or throw over the water, simply put your stroke back in the water at your shoulder.

Some students say it feels like the arm simply went up and down. For some, describing the arm action as extending a firm handshake or a punch. This drill is where you want to feel the beginning of some energy, power and athleticism in your swimming. It is OK to be tentative in feeling how far forward you can take your shoulder before it "locks up" and won't go any further forward. However, do not be tentative in your throw or thrusting of your stroke downwards with your weight. As one little boy described it, "My arm is the arrow entering the water and then my body becomes the arrow".

In the shoulder stroke drill, I want everyone to chop drop their strokes into the water. I want you to exaggerate the chop drop so you feel your weight dropping into the water with each stroke. After three or four shoulder strokes, you roll to your face up handle or backstroke drill position to inhale and assess how you did. Do the shoulder stroke drill as a drill and not a swim.

This drill will not feel as hard as swimming because your are propelling yourself by dropping your weight. Could work be any easier if work amounts to dropping your weight? Focus on dropping your weight more than working the row backwards.

The shoulder stroke drill is the last of my basic free style drills. With all drills, you want to see, exhale, have your weight over your chest, have your handle in front of you, throw before your row and take your throw directly to the "catch" or row ready position. Realistically, you can't think of all these actions at one time. My suggestion is to build upon the actions so they become automatic taking care of the highest priority needs first which are seeing and breathing.

Many coaches have used these drills in the past. What I hope you found to be new and helpful this time was the focus on your inner ear and seeing, breathing more often rather than less often, working with your flexibility and using your mass or weight to help you swim.

THE SIX FREESTYLE PERFROMANCE DRILLS ARE FAST HANDS, SHOULDER SHRUGS, SUPER GLIDES, DRUM BEATS, TREADMILL, AND SPACE CLAIMING.

When doing these drills, you are no longer rolling to your backstroke position to see, breathe and recover. By the time you begin these drills, you can see and breathe easily while swimming. You are going to swim these drills with two and three stroke swim patterns. Anyone looking at you would think that you are are just swimming. You are swimming in a way that takes aspects of your freestyle strokes and exaggerates them so you learn them well.

Do these drills for one pool length and then recover with backstroke or breaststroke on the return length. Recovery is important because recovery allows for greater exaggeration of focused effort. On days when you are not working solely on technique, you can still think of these drills while swimming and swim as far as you want with the drill in mind. On the days when you are time trialing in the water, it does pay to think of the drill you want for speed, energy conservation and efficiency while incorporate the drill into your swim.

You want to develop style and energy alternatives within freestyle. You will tire faster if you know how to only swim freestyle one way. If you can vary your freestyle, you can go farther and faster by using slightly different muscle groups or the same muscle groups at different angles of attack. Then when swimming conditions change due to waves or current for example, you can alter your freestyle stroke to better match the conditions.

These freestyle performance drills are more athletic and require more energy. These drills become your new tools to swim faster while learning the associated energy required.

ONE -Fast hands

Fast hands focuses on getting your hands to the front as fast as you can. There is no concern or emphasis on the row. You want a series of very fast throws. This is like sprinting for a length of the pool focusing on increasing the number of throws or strokes it takes to swim a length. For me, and many others, this drill requires a high energy output.

Your focus when throwing as fast as you can is to keep a "clean" hand entry that dives into the water without any sloppiness. When our hands are moving slow, we often don't notice that the hands are not entering the water properly. By speeding up the hands to sprint level and focusing on increasing the number of throws, we become aware of our sloppy hands. As you practice fast hands, you will notice some strokes hammering or slapping the water and some strokes knifing the water. You want each hand to feel like the point of a knife or arrow entering the water. You don't want to be slapping or hammering the water with your hands. At high speed, hammering or slapping hands are much more noticeable.

On land, the equivalent could be sprinting in place or sprinting fifty yards trying to increase your steps so you work on a fast foot action. Running coaches, especially sprint coaches, have their runners see how fast they can move the feet without worrying about stride length. I would like you to see how fast you can move your hands and arms without worrying about stroke length.

Be aware of the high energy cost of the fast hands drills. Yes, you could swim with fast hands, yet the energy cost is so high that you probably won't be able to sustain fast hands without eventually going anaerobic. You learn that there is more to swimming than just fast hands

With the fast hands drill do focus on how quickly you get to the next inhale. You will be inhaling every three strokes. You will have to exhale fast to have an inhale. No exhale means no inhale at these speeds. If you forget to exhale, then you will soon be out of breath. The fast hands drill also teaches you to speed up your exhale and inhale.

Focus on keeping an arm in front of you. Use the thumbs up technique when rolling for air to quicken the roll for air without impinging the shoulder.

Your body will be flatter in the water while going from side to side. Instead of a 45° angle, you may flatten out to a 15° angle on one side. Something has to give according to the laws of physics and what gives is body roll. Remember that if your body is at 15° then your hand will also be at a 15° angle leading the body. This is another difference between sprinters and distant swimmers in the water.

Sprinters tend to look flatter in the water while distance swimmers tend to roll more in the water. Like skaters, sprinters are more concerned with getting the action forward quickly while distance skaters are more concerned about creating a gliding action, on each side, for energy conservation.

As a distance swimmer, you don't want to lose awareness of having fast feet and sprinting. Even distance runners work on their sprinting to improve their technique and not lose a race after miles of running. Fast hands definitely feels like running, or sprinting, your stroke.

TWO - Shoulder shrugs

Shoulder shrugs are a low energy freestyle drill. I find it to be the lowest energy output of all of the drills. When swimming long distances, you might consider the focus of this drill to conserve your energy and give your arms a break.

Your focus is to swim with your shoulders and back as your deltoids lead your swim. The movement is like moving something large by putting your shoulder into it. Perhaps you can think of how football players, hockey players, wrestlers or basketball players use their shoulders when they move. Perhaps you can think of using your shoulder to move a large piece of furniture. Your shoulder is not going to be traveling far with a shrug. Yet, you are going to move a great deal of weight with each shrug using your deltoids and back muscles rather than your hands and arms.

Your hand and arm action is not going to fall apart though. Because, by the time you get to the performance drills, your hand and arm technique is rather automatic by now. Yet, don't think about your hands and arms. Imagine that you had no hands and arms, and you had to get from here to there by shrugging your shoulder in a deliberate, forward, rolling motion. It seems like you are inching along with your shoulders, yet the beauty and effect of the drill is that each forward shrug moves your weight forward with a low energy cost.

A benefit of the shoulder shrug drill is that it also has the effect of balancing your weight over your chest like the wheelbarrow drill did. Your shoulders are neither high nor low in the water. Shrugging your shoulders tends to keep your weight level and driving forward with an effective weight transfer.

Having focused on seeing, breathing, kicking and your hands and arms, it can be a challenge to stop thinking about those actions (which are very high priority actions) and solely focus on a shoulder shrug. With three strokes before your inhale, you want to feel three distinct, deliberate shoulder shrugs before your inhale. Like fast hands, the shoulder shrug is a three stroke drill. Yet, unlike fast hands, shoulder strokes could be a walking or running rhythm stroke drill.

THREE - Super glides.

Super glides are a two stroke drill. If you are swimming a long distance, you might use two stroke swimming to see often, breathe often and glide more. Your swimming action can become similar to a distance skater who takes more advantage of their glide.

The focus when you are trying to glide through the water is attempting to cross the pool in one stroke. I know that is impossible without the help of kicking or dolphining; yet, make each throw, row and glide combination as if you are trying to cross the pool in one stroke. With each stroke have a forceful throw that initiates a forceful row that continues with a strong glide helped by maintaining a streamline with arm extension and full core strength. When your momentum has slowed, take another stroke to see if you can finish crossing the pool with the next stroke.

Do not kick when gliding other than the single kick that you take when you throw your hand and arm into the water. You want the focus to be on a powerful throw, row and glide action. Do not distract yourself with kicking or propelling yourself with kicking. You want to isolate this drill to your upper body and core.

If this were skating, the focus would be to see how far you could get with a single skate and glide. It would take power and then holding your line for a long glide to cross the ice in one skating action.

With two stroke swimming, you breathe every other stoke. Many people breathe every two strokes or every four stroke because "they can't" breathe to the other side as well. The base freestyle drills will have you rolling up and down on both sides. By the time you begin performance drills, be able to breathe to either side, your left or your right.

Breathing to your left and to your right means that you will be breathing towards the same wall or the same direction as you swim back and forth. You breathe to your left on the way down and you breathe to your right on the way back keeping your face to the same wall and working both sides of your body. Somewhat surprisingly, many experienced swimmers make faster gains on their "weak" side where "they can't" breathe because they do not have to forget or overcome muscle memory on that side.

You want to be able to swim with combinations of two strokes and three strokes. Two strokes lets you see more, breathe more and glide more (if you want). Three strokes allows you to switch the side you were breathing and seeing towards. Three strokes allows you to see to your left and right so you can choose the optimal side to see and breathe towards if you want to go to a two or four stroke pattern. Three stroke swimming allows you to "run" your stroke. If you are under 150 pounds, you probably prefer to take more strokes faster (velocity) to make up for your lack of weight (mass) to keep your speed (momentum) where you want it to be. It's a one two three, one two three pattern similar to a waltz. While most of my performance stroke drills are three stroke drills, bounding or super glides is a two stroke drill. I do swim more than two thirds of the time with a two stroke pattern while also applying the focus of three stroke drills to my two stroke swimming.

With the super glide drill, you are going for energy, athleticism and possibly even a resting glide. In fact, please keep the drill from becoming swimming by using a resting glide. Allow your body to slow down during the glide so you have to overcome some inertia each time you take a powerful throw and row. Feel like you are skating through the water and not running fast or swimming when doing this drill.

FOUR - Drum beat rows

After the bounding or super glide drill, you re-learn the importance of a good row. So far, I have not had a drill on the row because most people come with too much row, row, row.

The row or "catch and pull" as swimmers refer to it is greatly overrated and dissected by opinionated swimmers. When there is film or video or a picture of someone swimming, most of the discussion centers around the hand and arm that rows or "catches and pulls" in the water. Some people will go on and on about fingers apart or together, a flat hand or a cupped hand, forearm position, elbow position and how far the pull should last, go backwards or come out of the water. These discussions are as bad as political parties arguing about how you should crack an egg open. Anything that I write about the row or catch and pull will be eviscerated by one side or the other.

I teach swimmers to begin with a straight arm row when drilling or swimming unless they come to me with a good row. A straight arm row is like an oar in the water under you. It is straight and strong. The straight arm row builds functional strength at your arm pit, shoulder and upper arm. If you don't have strength there, your row will be a weak row. A straight arm throw breaks the bad habit of leading with your elbow during your row. A straight arm through the water is the simplest progression towards a row where there is some bend at the elbow.

A straight arm row is also a good row if you have swimmer's elbow. Tennis players, golfers and swimmers can develop a sore elbow from overuse or improper technique. A bent elbow allows for more strain at the elbow when you bend the elbow. If you are suffering from swimmer's elbow, try a straighter row, like an oar rowing to lessen the strain on your elbow. You can simply try this with a table in front of you, bend your elbow and push downwards like you do swimming. Then compare how your elbow feels when you straighten the arm and push down. If you are like me, you won't feel the pain and strain with the straight arm row.

The drum beat row is a progression in developing your underwater rowing action. Rather than a straight arm row, have your elbow bend as if you are playing a drum at your waist. Your hand and forearm go from the extended, thumbs up position that matches your body angle, to a flat hand and forearm leading the row back to your waist and then your front thigh where you drilled with your hand on your thigh in the wheelbarrow and handle drills. You are now building functional strength at your elbow and wrist. By leading the row with your forearm, you are making your elbow work by staying in place and engaged. By leading the row with your hand, you are making your wrist work.

If you really do the drum beat row well, the bottom of your hand muscles, your oppenens digiti minimi, will be worked like the blade of an ice skate turning to catch the ice so you can have a solid push off on a slippery surface like ice or water.

Your hand can be flat or cupped. Your fingers can be together or apart. A problem that I sometimes see with a flat hand is that some swimmers allow the flat hand to flare up, back or outwards catching water the wrong way. The hand that signals "stop" slows you down. Imagine a French police office stopping traffic with his hand motion. Sometimes swimmers don't notice that their flat hand is flaring up, back or out slowing their swim. For this reason, I tend to prefer a slightly cupped hand as if someone is pouring water into your hand.

The chain of functional strength for a good rowing action is actually at your leverage points and not the muscles themselves. You first need leverage where the shoulder and upper arm meet (arm pit), then leverage at your elbow and then at your wrist. When doing weight lifting and resistance stretching for swimming, it's inaccurate to gauge your functional strength in the water by what a muscle can lift. While your back muscles, triceps and forearm may be strong, if you don't have functional strength at your joints, you can't use your muscle strength. Swimming strength for long distances is more like lifting ten to thirty pound weights a thousand times or more. You don't swim at full muscular strength. You swim at full joint or leverage strength, so keep this in mind when lifting weights and doing resistance stretching. Work your levers or joints and not just individual muscles.

The angle of your row is also important. Of course, a flat surface, hand, forearm and upper arm is superior to angling that flat surface in the water. If you angle your hand and arm, then your row is going to slip in the water. However, your row slipping in the water is not the end of the world though. It's detrimental; but, it is not the end of life as we know it. If your row is angled and slipping in the water, your technique could be bad or you could be tiring as you swim. It is common for all athletes to alter their stride, change the gears, use a different club or alter their swim stroke as they tire. Be aware of a flat row, yet if you have to angle your arm like a propeller blade or wing angles to function, do so. Besides rowing, you are propelling yourself with throwing and kicking. If the equivalent of a thirty pound row becomes to difficult to maintain, switch to a ten or twenty pound row by angling your arm.

The drum beat is a three stroke drill. Do three good drum beat like rows before you inhale. I like to think of drummers from Scotland or England that drum by going from full arm extension to a solid bent arm drum beat and then back to full arm extension. When doing the drum beat drill you do want to maintain your arm in front of you leading your swim until it is time to row. Then you focus on the row which consists of functional strength at your joints with the bottom of your hand catching or digging the water like a skate does on ice.

Remember that a good throw initiates a good row. Don't neglect a good throw, but once you throw work your drum beat like row that really catches the water like an ice skate catches the ice while skating.

FIVE - Treadmill

The treadmill drill is another fast hands out of the water drill. Perhaps, it is most like the way people swim. The focus is bringing the hand more quickly from your thigh to the water in front of you. You are trying to gain speed and momentum where it is easiest, in the air, with what they call the recovering arm. I would rather you not think of your arm as"recovering" as it moves through the air during this drill. Your arm could be fast and more efficiently at work by running to the front. The arm in the air creates forward momentum that offers a 100% return on effort.

Your arm in the air will move faster than your row in the water in this drill. Your arm extended in front of you will still remain there (recovering in my view) until the throwing hand arrives on the scene. You are not focusing on rowing faster. The hand and arm in the air is on the treadmill moving faster than the hand and arm in the water. Your arm in the air hurries back to the front trying to pick up speed as if the hand and arm were trying to keep up with a fast moving treadmill.

Keeping your finger tips on the water's surface enhances this drill. Your fingers on the water's surface can give you a feel for how fast your arm is moving and helps create the low throw that you want with the treadmill drill. Your focus is not bounding which emphasizes a powerful throw into the water. Your focus is more like running with a fast and low to the ground shuttle, like you would do in longer running races to save your legs.

Like fast hands, your body tends to flatten out and roll from side to side less. So rather than a 45° roll to one side, you might only roll 30° to each side for a total of 60° degrees of face down rolling. Your thumbs up hand position will be at the angle that your body is in the water, so your hand will be at 30°.

The treadmill drill is not a sprint. The treadmill drill is at race pace or a little faster. While the fast hands drill feels like a sprint, keep the treadmill drill fast like your tempo for a race.

As a three stroke pattern, you want to feel like you are quickly getting to your next inhale. If you don't hurry your strokes up during when taking three strokes, you are breathing farther apart than you would with your two stroke pattern and you will tire from not having enough oxygen. When taking three strokes, do not try to maintain a two stroke distance. You are varying your stroke to divide the same amount of work into three parts rather that two. Of course, we would like two stroke distance with three stroke swimming, yet physically something has to give.

You could use the treadmill drill when swimming against a current. It is advantageous to emphasize hurrying the arm out the water where it is not fighting the water current. Try to think of every break that you can create for yourself as water conditions vary.

SIX - Space claiming

Perhaps my favorite performance drill is space claiming. In my mind, the space claiming drill is right up there with bounding or super glide. Space claiming is a three stroke drill. Your focus is keeping your arms in front of you to claim the space in front of you where your body is going.

As a triathlete and open water swimmer, it is important for me to stake out or claim the water or space in front of me. It is my space where I am going. The only way to do this is by having my arms in front of me. Other swimmers are not going to know that this is my space unless I have something there to claim it. Sometimes triathletes and open water swimmers complain about getting kicked in the head and losing their goggles. The fault is really their own because they were leading with their head rather than their hands and arms. If the hands and arms had been leading their swim and claiming that space in front of them, then they would not have been kicked in the head. Instead, they would have annoyed the swimmer in front of them by touching the feet of the swimmer in front, giving the swimmer in front the correct impression that someone was about to pass them.

Space claiming is a relatively fast and streamlined three stroke swimming drill. Keeping a hand and arm in front of you means being fast and diligent in getting your arm back in front of you while maintaining your other arm in front of you. Keeping an extended hand and arm in front of you translates into a continuous level core engaged streamline as you swim. This drill is very efficient as you receive more than one benefit from practicing it.

This is not the "catch-up drill" that some swimmers do. I avoid the catch-up drill altogether because it does not teach a swimmer when to time their weight shift. Even though it teaches keeping an arm in front of you, you need the next step too. Space claiming allows your weight and momentum to transfer at the last moment in front of you rather than catch-up and stop.

A challenge that develops with space claiming and keeping the extension and streamline going a little longer is that your stroke length becomes a little longer and your inhales are therefore a little farther apart. As you develop fitness though, you might develop a longer exhale followed by the quick look and inhale needed to facilitate claiming the space in front of you. It is easier to feel that you are claiming the space in front of you when you are not rolling up and down to breathe. Yet, you want to be so good at swimming that the difference between a stroke where you are inhaling and a stroke where you are exhaling becomes less and less over time.

If you race in the pool, you know that it is the first hand that reaches the wall that wins. Therefore, competitive swimmers swim to the wall trying to touch the wall with a throw rather than taking a row close to the wall. In the the space claiming drill, swim as if the wall is right there in front of you. You're trying to keep your hands and arms moving forward so you touch before your competition does.

Keeping your arms extended and streamlined, helps to level the rest of your body. By keeping your hand and arm streamlined, the result is that the other ninety percent of your body becomes streamlined, too. The arm is extended just below your chest in the ready to "catch and pull" or row position yet you are not contracting to row. Instead, you are extending your as hand and arm as if a water fairy was holding your hand and pulling you through the water with your handle. If you are a big swimmer, you might need to imagine a mermaid holding your hand and pulling you. Use the image of someone taking your hand and pulling it through the water while your hand is extended in the thumbs up hand shake position. The arm in this position below your chest, also accurately positions your body's weight over the front wheel of your wheelbarrow, at your pectoral muscle.

Space claiming tends to get you back to more of a 45° roll to the left and then 45° to the right. Whatever angle you want your body to roll from side to side, keep the angle of your hand at the same angle to facilitate the roll to your side creating a better keel. Again, keeping hand and body in agreement with your body is also shoulder neutral and protects your shoulders and rotator cuff.

Now that you know of several freestyle drills, you can put together a highly technical swim for a half hour or more making detailed technical gains with your swim stroke while gaining fitness.

Chapter Fifteen – Workouts and Training.

Comparing sprint training (intervals) to distance training.

From the studies that I have read, there are more health benefits to aerobic training, especially as you age. The body becomes less able to handle the byproducts of hard anaerobic (without oxygen) work as you age. Recovery from anaerobic work is a requirement and not an option. More aerobic recovery occurs while you train and the way you recover from anaerobic training is aerobic. There will be times when you train aerobically that you will go anaerobic and that is all the anaerobic training you will need.

You can still go hard for short distances to maintain strength, flexibility and speed and yet have aerobic workouts. Twenty-five yards in a pool is about thirty seconds and you generally don't go into deep oxygen debt, swimming anaerobically, if you limit it to twenty-five yards or less. Short, faster bursts build you up. Long, hard intervals that leave you feeling worse for the wear during, after and days after your workout are to be avoided.

Aerobic training does not have to be slow. Some people say that an aerobic pace is seventy percent of your target heart rate. I don't train aerobically at seventy percent, unless I am recovering. I can go much higher with a heart rate of 160 for a fifty-six year old man and keep it going for hours. Aerobic training is actually the fastest pace that you can maintain beyond twenty minutes. There could be as little as a few seconds per hundred yards between your aerobic and anaerobic pace, so aerobic swimming is not slow, it's fast without the lactic acid. And, as you adapt aerobically, your fast aerobic pace per hundred yards will increase surpassing what used to be your fast anaerobic pace.

There are several problems training at an anaerobic pace. Lactic acid and other byproducts of anaerobic training increase anxiety. The byproducts of anaerobic training have to processed by your body creating greater demands on your organs. Anaerobic combustion is limited to about fifteen minutes and after fifteen minutes you return to an aerobic or recovery state unable to go further anaerobically. Technique tends to suffer as it is hard to maintain technique when you are out of breath, hurting and anxious.

If you are training to be the top athlete in your high school, college, country or the world, you do need anaerobic training after you laid down a solid aerobic base. Training for your health and age group placement in races, really does not require anaerobic training. There are plenty of people you can beat without breaking your breathing pattern and going anaerobic.

Because there are so many positive benefits of aerobic workouts and so many negatives for anaerobic workouts, I recommend that you raise your aerobic threshold by training aerobically ninety percent of the time. The other ten percent will be short speed work that does not become fully anaerobic and some inadvertent anaerobic training. As a distance athlete, ninety percent or more of your race is going to be aerobic once you go beyond twenty minutes. Therefore, your results for twenty minutes or more improve by raising your aerobic level and improving your technique. Don't be satisfied with a slow aerobic pace or poor technique. Continue to adopt a faster aerobic pace and maintain stroke quality as your fitness increases.

Flip turns and workouts

You will be doing right side up flip turns during your the workouts. In effect, you will be swimming your entire workout without stopping unless you have to go to the bathroom or adjust your goggles. The sooner that you do stop standing on the bottom of the pool, the better. When swimming outdoors in a river, lake or ocean, you can't assume that you will be able to stop and stand up.

Right side up flip turns have you face up on the surface of the water, seeing upwards, breathing, tucking forward, seeing the lane in front of you and then further tucking under the water and pushing off the wall. I think the traditional face down in the water flip turn of going without an inhale while tucking and not seeing the lane in front of you are wrong side down flip turns. I am not even certain which turn is faster and it doesn't really matter to me; because, I know I will never do a wrong side down flip turn in a triathlon or open water swim. Yet, you could do a right side up flip turn in a triathlon. So why do wrong side down flip turns unless you are going to compete in short sprint races in a pool and you can't take the peer pressure of being different.

The benefits of a right side flip turn are: you won't be putting your feet on the bottom of the pool which builds your confidence in your ability to swim long distances; you get a breath of air versus missing a breath of air; you get to see the lane in front of you so you don't tuck and push off the wall into another swimmer. The tuck is the same whether you are doing it right side up or wrong side down.

One further important benefit is that many pools are about three feet deep at the wall. It is far safer to do a right side up flip turn with your head out of the water in three feet of water. It is not safe to do a wrong side down flip turn and hit your head on the bottom of the pool. And, the older you are, the more of a problem wrong side down flip turns are for an adult's head and inner ear if you are not already used to it.

Recovery workouts

The top priority of a recovery swim is recovery so don't make it work. A recovery swim can last ten minutes or less. After a hard bike, run or day at work, it is worthwhile to go to the pool for ten minutes to recover.

While doing a recovery swim, just swim and focus on seeing and good exhale. You want to get rid of the tension, carbon dioxide, and by products of training in your blood stream though exhalation. A long, slow, complete exhale underwater will help you recover and no one will notice your deep underwater exhales and sighs.

As you swim, the pressure from the water on your legs will help the body return blood to your heart. The water pressure helps venous blood flow back to your heart by ten percent, simply by the water pressure on your body. That the legs are also level with your heart, helps your blood flow from your legs and organs to your heart.

The cooling effect of the water helps the body cool. It is embarrassing to return sweating after a workout. This is not the case after a cool down, recovery swim that returns your body temperature to normal.

While cooling down for ten minutes to recover, if you can notice improvements in your ability to see, breathe and technique, all the better.

Remember, you are recovering for the sake of your next workout. You are not swimming for the sake of improving or continuing that day's workout, so make your recovery swims easy.

Technical workouts

Ten minute warmup.
Ten minutes of base drills.
Ten minutes of performance drills.
Swim after drilling to lengthen your technical workout.

Technical workouts work your technique. The workouts are like going to the driving range and putting green to improve your golf game. Golfers go the driving range and putting greens to practice their technique for more practice than playing a round of golf offers. Tennis players also set aside time to practice aspects of their serve or volley. Tennis players might practice just their serve for a half hour before working their forehand and backhand returns. It is not uncommon for professional golfers and tennis players to practice more than they play. Your technical workouts are not distance swims or intervals. Your technical workouts isolate seeing, breathing, weight positioning, kicking, throwing and rowing so you improve your technique in each of these areas.

When doing a technical swim, make it the first workout in your training day. Do not do a technical workout after weightlifting, cycling or running as your tiredness and physical stiffness negatively influences quality. Notice the degradation of your technique after cycling or running for the information that it offers in your recovery swim. Yet, it is less than ideal to work on your technique when you arrive tired. I recommend that you do a technical swim followed by weightlifting to stretch your muscles, improve your core strength, and balance muscle strength.

Ten minute warmup.

Warm up by swimming for ten minutes. Your ten minute warm up swim is not a time trial to check your race pace. Your warm up swim is a wake up swim. At five in the morning or at five in the afternoon, you need to wake up so you can pay attention to your technique. The goal of a warm up swim is to get you sweating. While you can't see yourself sweat in a pool, if the water no longer feels cool or cold and if your body feels warm, you have warmed up. On average, out of the water, it takes about ten minutes to break a sweat while cycling, running or walking. It takes about the same amount of time in the water to wake up and warm up.

Swim as you want for the ten minute warmup. Hard core swimmers may do a thousand yards in ten minutes of freestyle. Soft core swimmers may do ten minutes of backstroke, breaststroke and freestyle all mixed together so they don't feel exhausted after a "warm up". One of the unfortunate aspects of some masters' swim teams workouts is that some beginners feel exhausted (and nearly drowned) after the "warm up" with experienced swimmers. For myself, I like to do a length of three stroke freestyle, followed by two lengths of two stroke freestyle to warm up rolling to my left for one length and my right for one length, followed by a length of backstroke to engage my core and work my kick. I repeat this one hundred yard routine for ten minutes.

Your warm can be a good diagnostic tool to focus on an aspect or several aspects of your technique that you notice at this time. That would be like playing nine holes of golf and then going to the driving range immediately to work on your technique. If you notice technical problems while warming up, make certain that your swim drills address your concerns.

Ten minutes of base drills.

Kicking drills are good place to begin drilling. Kicking drills have you on your back, half of the time and face down half of the time so seeing and breathing is less of an issue. You practice during the kicking drills rolling down and the very important rolling up for air. You practice positioning your weight on the front wheel of your wheelbarrow (upper chest and upper back). You practice engaging your lowest abdominal muscles. You practice a forward swimmer's kick and not a backward runner's kick. You keep your weight on your front wheel so your weight does not go to your waist, where you weight is wasted. You practice freestyle when face down and backstroke when face up. You really can accomplish a great deal technically without even taking a stroke.

The wheelbarrow kicking drill is the most challenging of the two kicking drills. Without your arm and hand to help handle your weight, it is pretty much weight positioning, neck flexibility, core strength and a forward kick moving you through the water. If you can do the wheelbarrow kicking drill correctly, you are far ahead of most people, swimmers included.

After doing the wheelbarrow for a pool length, swim back a length, focusing on keeping your weight positioned correctly at your chest, under your arm pit and then your scapula as you swim and roll for air. I would focus on weight positioning, breathing and seeing before I would focus on kicking as you swim back. How much and how hard you must kick is a result of how poorly your weight is positioned. The better that you position your weight, the less you will have to kick to compensate for poor technique.

Many distance swimmers and triathletes want to "stop" or limit kicking and do no more than one kick for one arm entry (swimmers call it the two beat kick to further confuse anti-swimmers) to save their legs. My kicking drills could lead to the "end of all kicking". While working your kick you learn to position your weight and build your core so much so that kicking isn't any more important to swimming than your arms are to running. Imagine the horror if we had to six beat kick our arms while running to compensate for not being able to position our weight correctly while walking or running. If you position your weight and engage your core, you can

141

swim without a kick much like you can swim with a pull buoy between your legs that prevents you from kicking while swimming.

However, if you need your kick to keep your momentum going in between strokes, keep kicking. I am not urging small swimmers (especially children) to stop kicking. Small swimmers, who lack mass, must make up for their lack of mass by kicking so their momentum does not drop quickly in between strokes. For small and large swimmers my kicking drills improves their kick in the freestyle and backstroke position that they will swim. Swim a length after you kick a length to gain from your kicking drills.

The handle drill is the next kicking drill that you work. While actually easier than the wheelbarrow drill because the arm and hand set the tone and lead the body, I do the handle kicking drill as a progression towards your stroke drills. Keep in mind the technical improvements that the wheelbarrow drill offered and include using your handle for additional technical improvements. Your handle helps you position your weight on one breast when you are face down and on one scapula when you are face up on your back. Your handle helps you streamline by extending the arm and hand. Imagine someone pulling your hand and arm so you feel pulled in the water. Extending you arm deliberately creates a taut arm that creates a tauter body that bends less at the waist helping you to keep your weight at your chest and not at your waist where your weight is wasted. Your hand angled on its side, and not flat, helps your body be angled on its side from your pinky, to your ilia crest, to your little toe. Your hand and arm also lead your body in the all important roll up for an inhale. If you leave your hand and arm behind, flat in the water, it's about as awkward as being left on the dance floor. You learn in the handle drill that the arm leads the body and that whatever you want the body to do, have the arm do it first to lead the way.

Do a length of the handle drill. And, then swim back a length rolling up for air with the same hand and arm motion that you used when you rolled up for air when not taking a stroke. While you swim, use your handle to help you lead the roll for air. The bad habit, that you will breaking with this technique is pushing down on a liquid in order to raise a solid. Pushing down on a liquid to raise a solid doesn't work very well for very long. Rolling a solid in the water, works much better. Use small levers like your hand and arm rolling thumbs up so your body follows and rolls, too. While swimming back, your primary focus is your hand and arm leading and maintaining the body's roll for air. Like the handle drill, the longer you maintain your weight positioned and arm extend, the longer you can inhale without sinking at your wasteful waist.

When you swim back, swim with a two stroke pattern because you want to maximize the number of times you roll for air, while keeping your arm on the side you drilled extended while inhaling. It is better to practice your rolling for air ten times with two stroke swimming, than to practice just five rolls for air with four stroke swimming. You may not like the mistakes you make when rolling for air, yet you will get better by improving the errors of your ways with more practice closer together. Do not do three stroke swimming on the way back as alternating your roll for air from the left to right, means that it will take six strokes to get back to correcting a mistake you noticed on your left or right side, six strokes ago.

Doing the handle kicking drill requires that you do at least two lengths of the handle drill. One length is for your left handle. After that length, swim back with two stroke swimming. Another length is for your right handle. After that length, swim back with two stroke swimming. You want to practice with your left arm leading during the drill the entire length and then swimming back with your left arm leading the body's roll for air (rolling right). Then you want to practice your right arm leading the kicking drill for a pool length followed by swimming with the right arm leading the body's roll to air (rolling left).

The handle kicking drill is an invaluable kicking drill. This is the one drill to emphasize more than the other drills. Most swimmers slow down while swimming when they roll for a breath of air due to poor technique. For that reason many sprinters in the water try not breathe or try to limit the number of breaths they take. Distance swimmers and triathletes can not afford to run out of air. If you need to breathe, to swim your race distance, practice your roll for air until you no longer slow down nor momentarily have to increase your effort after inhaling to get back up to speed.

Two stroke swimming, and being able breathe left for one length and right for another length, is a drill in and of itself that challenges you to get "it" right stroke after stroke. If you can swim as fast with two stroke swimming as you can with three stroke swimming, or vice versa, you have made a lot of progress.

The next drill to practice is the underwater swimming drill to begin improving your stroke timing and weight transfer in front of you. During this stroke drill, you keep your handle extended until the forward motion of your throwing arm is parallel to your forearm and wrist which then initiates the row. It's the throw before you row. Feel your weight tipping easily in front of you at arms length. If you can't feel the moment your weight has tipped or transferred from one side and to the other, you are not doing the drill correctly and perhaps too fast to feel the tipping moment.

The underwater swimming drill has your row at its maximum length. Your row begins at the point of your extended handle and rows back to the front of your thigh. While swimming your row might not be that long, yet while doing the underwater swimming drill, be able to touch the front of your thigh to know how long your row could be. After the weight exchange in front of you, the rowing arm is no longer the body's primary weight bearing arm. On the way back to your thigh, the rowing arm is your propulsive arm at that time in the stroke sequence.

The underwater drill is usually a three stroke drill, yet could be done as a two or four stroke drill if you want to isolate certain aspects of the weight transfer and long row. Some people have only enough of an exhale to do two underwater strokes and I would rather you do two unhurried strokes than three hurried strokes. A common mistake to avoid in doing stroke drills is not to take five, six or seven strokes before rolling breathless and anxious up to backstroke position to kick, inhale and regroup. The problem with taking too many strokes is that stroke number four, five and six tend to be hurried and of a lower quality because you are running out of oxygen. So instead of your last memory being two or three good strokes, your last memory is two or three poor, hurried strokes. Remember to drill your drills and not swim your drills.

You swim a length after you drill a length with the underwater swimming drill. As you swim back, can you keep your handle extended until the throwing arm enters the water and your weight shifts in front you? While swimming back, inhale every third stroke if you can, and feel that one arm is always claiming the space in front of you where your body is going. The swim back is much like the space claiming performance drill without being at race pace. Do not hurry the swim back because you want to really feel your weight exchanging in front of you and not under you. Pay attention to your handle leading your roll to air and remaining in front of you when you roll back down so that you never go without an arm in front of your head, protecting your head and enhancing your stroke quality.

The shoulder stroke drill is usually a three stroke drill. You want to feel your weight dropping or diving into the water with each throw. While drilling feel your weight propelling you with the arm dropping or diving into the water so the effort of your row is secondary. Your row will still look good and feel good because your throw dropped your weight into the water at the correct angle. Again, do three strong throws with your elbow extended away from your body and forearm perpendicular to the water, at your shoulder and not your head, and then roll to your backstroke position for a good break before your practice three more strokes. You might only drill nine strokes in a twenty-five yard length, which is fine.

Swim a length back after you drill a length with shoulder strokes. When you swim back, feel the power of your arm that is out of the water going directly into the water like you are reaching for treasure below the water's surface. Be like a greedy pirate after the gold as you reach with a determined stroke into the water. We are talking about free treasure below the surface if you just drop the weight of your arm and your back to that side. Don't make dropping your weight less effective by lowering your arm slowly. Don't make it hard by being tentative and resisting your arm diving and falling into the water to reap the treasure of speed without much effort.

Ten minutes of performance drills

Freestyle performance drills are done at race pace effort (or faster). Because these drills are done at full effort, only do them for one length. After you swim your freestyle performance drill at full effort, do the advanced elementary backstroke, breaststroke or Olympic style backstroke for one length on the way back to practice those strokes and recover. Once recovered, you can go at full effort again, with the same or another freestyle performance drill.

Besides recovery, an efficient breaststroke allows you to see straight ahead while catching your breath and giving your freestyle muscles a break. When swimming in the open water, we repeat a pattern of freestyle then breaststroke and back to freestyle. In effect, we are creating a pool wall in the open water. You can swim a number of freestyle strokes, dependent on your ability, followed by a number of breaststrokes. Some swimmers do four and four. Some swimmers do eight freestyle strokes and two breaststrokes followed by eight freestyle strokes (which for many people is about twenty-five yards). The breaststroke fits into the strategy of not going off course nor letting your freestyle stroke deteriorate. The breaststroke kick also keeps anyone who is about to swim over you, swimming around you. Develop your recovery breaststroke when doing freestyle performance drills.

Fast hands is a good performance drill to begin the performance drills. Fast hands is like a sprint focusing solely on fast throws and clean hand entries in the water. You need to exhale fast because the next inhale is coming fast. If you can keep a clean hand entry at sprint speed, you will notice a sloppy hand entry at slower speeds. Your hands and forearms knife the water and not hammer or slap the water.

Swim back with a recovery backstroke or breaststroke. Catch your breath. Relax for a length because you will be going at full effort again.

Shoulder shrugs is a good performance drill to follow fast hands. Your shoulders and back muscles are doing the work allowing your hands and forearms to recover even more. You will probably notice an exponential energy difference between fast hands and shoulder shrugs. You might come to the right conclusion that when you are tired, shoulder shrugs are efficient.

Swim back with a recovery backstroke or breaststroke. Catch your breath. Relax for a length because you will be going at full effort again.

Super glides are what I like to do next in the series of my performance drills. Every throw, row and glide combination exudes power and athleticism. The action is like a power lift in weight lifting or dunking the basketball. Each stroke is its own score and you are focused solely on the powerful stroke that you are taking. While the throw and row are high energy, the extension and glide is like recovery. This stroke is like taking long strides while skating to eat up the distance. You will probably take the fewest number of strokes to cross the pool with this drill.

Swim back with a recovery backstroke or breaststroke. Catch your breath. Relax for a length because you will be going at full effort again.

Remember that you only did the left side with super glides so when you return, you will be doing super glides on your right side.

Swim back one length with a recovery backstroke or breaststroke. Catch your breath. Relax for a length because you will be going at full effort again.

After feeling the strong row in the super glides, I like to follow up with the drum beat drill. The drum beat drill is a three stroke drill so feel three distinct drum beat like rows before looking for an inhale.

Swim back with a recovery backstroke or breaststroke. Catch your breath. Relax for a length because you will be going at full effort again.

Next, I do the treadmill drill. I want to get back to the arms running forward in the air while the fingers touch the surface of the water. The fingers on the water give me feedback on arm speed and an arm throw that is close to the surface. Run the fingers forward like a treadmill works at race pace breathing every three strokes to get the correct results.

Swim back a length with a recovery backstroke or breaststroke. Catch your breath. Relax for a length because you will be going at full effort again.

At the end of the performance drills, I prefer the space claiming performance drill. For me, space claiming and super glides is what I like to go towards on race day. Space claiming claims the space in front of my head to protect me. Space claiming is fast because I am staking out my claim on the space where I am swimming. The drill keeps an arm extended so I stay streamlined, too.

Swim back with a recovery backstroke or breaststroke. Catch your breath. Relax for a length because you will be going at full effort again.

If you are able, you might do more that one set of the performance drill series. When I have time, I like to work on the performance drill that felt great or rework the drill that did not feel so great. It's your choice on days that you are doing technical swims, to determine how much you want to hone your skill.

Time Trials

Time trials are used to measure your progress and determine your race pace. Intervals, because of the rest interval, are not good indicators of your speed over your race distance. It is a common mistake to feel that your interval pace could be your race pace and start out too fast in a race. Time trials, at your race distance, help you better judge your pace from the beginning of the race. The beginning of the race is the most important part of the race to be on pace.

Too many athletes, in general, go out too fast in their races. The adrenaline of the starting line, has some people sprinting at a pace that they can't keep up for four minutes, let alone fourteen or forty minutes. Starting too fast demonstrates Lydiard's point that most people are fast enough, they just lack endurance. While your body can swim the first twenty-five yards fast, and not go anaerobic, few people are disciplined enough to get back to race pace after a fast start. And, even if you do get back to race pace after your fast start, you still could have those swimmers sprinting for four minutes swimming over you. Yet, you can control your pace and the technique of keeping your arms in front of you, while swimming, to have a good race start. And, once the race is spreads out, fewer swimmers will be next to you and you will be able to swim your own race.

When doing a time trial in training, the middle of your time trial, gives you a realistic sense of your pace. If you began swimming at two minutes per hundred yards and then slow down and swim at two minutes and ten seconds per hundred yards, your pace is two minutes and ten seconds and not the two minutes per hundred.

A big aid to swimming a time trial well is thinking about your technique during the time trial. If you concentrate your thoughts on the effort it is taking, the time trial could feel arduous. It is better for you if you think of one or two of your favorite techniques: streamlining, bounding, claiming the space in front of you, shoulder shrugs, weight positioned at your chest, etc. in order to hold your pace or perhaps improve your pace. You're really on the right track if your hundred yard segments speed up due to improved technique rather than more effort.

Measure your time trials in segment of a hundred yards or more. Quickly look at your watch, after doing a right side up flip turn, to determine how much time the last hundred took. You might lose a half second in taking that look, yet the pace information is invaluable while you are time time trialing. In many triathlons, buoys are also one or two hundred yards apart and you could quickly look at your watch too see how fast you are swimming while racing. It is important to know if you are gaining or losing seconds as you swim. Once you know what is working well (technique) and what is not working well (unsustainable effort), you can decide how you want to swim the next hundred yards.

Practice sighting or seeing where you are going while swimming your time trials. Site at least once a length to practice seeing and breathing. Some swimmers site while swimming freestyle. I think this favors the bigger swimmers whose mass keeps them going in the water better than small swimmers. Using the breaststroke to site is also an alternative. The breaststroke allows you to see better, breathe better, and rest your freestyle muscles which is an attractive combination.

An open water swim, especially in triathlons where the swimmers' experience levels vary so much, is like playing a timed round of golf. Instead of a swim, what if they set off waves of golfers for nine or eighteen holes and then had you get on your bike. While as ridiculous and dangerous as that sounds, there are people who would prefer a round of golf over a swim to start a triathlon. Like swimming, it would not matter if you had one good hole or one good shot. It would matter if you had straight, sustainable series of good strokes that got you through the course quickly and easily.

When doing time trials weekly measure your progress. Reliably dropping your hundreds by an average of one second is not insignificant if the effort felt the same and your technique better. It is better to steadily lower your times than to have your times go back and forth. Time trials are for self knowledge, so don't race them, learn from them throughout the year. Time trials have you swimming your own race so do them on weekends when you don't have a race.

Chapter Sixteen – Racing

Racing outdoors is quite different than swimming indoors. Your ability to see is lessened which results in some anxiety which could make breathing more of a problem too, until you get used to the situation. Anyone who grew up swimming outdoors wonders what all the fuss is about swimming outdoors. They are not bothered by not being able to see underwater any further than their arm. They look where they are going when they want. They change swim strokes when they want while swimming. They take some pleasure in the discomfort that others feel outdoors because that is to their advantage. On the other hand, if you are an adult who only knows swimming pools, the change to a lake, river or ocean is significant. The more you practice seeing more often, breathing more and changing strokes in the middle of the pool, then you will be better prepared for the outdoors.

Most people race alone and don't plan on using anyone else while racing. Their plan is to start off to the side, in the back, or in the front if they are strong swimmers and swim their own race as if no one else is swimming. While that approach sounds good, it seldom happens. Other swimmers may follow you thinking that you are a good swimmer to follow. The fact that everyone is swimming to the same buoys and that there are more swimmers behind you coming in waves means that you won't truly be racing alone. You might feel alone, as if the next swimmer wouldn't notice if you were drowning, yet you are seldom alone unless you are one of the last people in the water.

Racing with others is a better strategy. If it is inevitable that you are going to be racing with others, plan on using their somewhat predictable behaviors to help your race. Predictable behaviors vary depending on the skill level of the swimmers that surround you. Competent swimmers at the front of the pack have seeing and breathing under control and swim at a steadier pace. On the other hand, barely competent swimmers often zigzag while swimming and will stop and tread water to see and breathe. Then there is the range of swimmers in between the very competent and the barely competent where we find ourselves swimming.

While racing with others, you want to swim with swimmers of your level or better, yet you also want to pass less competent swimmers while using their behaviors to help you get ahead too. Swimming in a pack of swimmers is like running or cycling in a pack of people. While you don't want to feel boxed in and unable to move and being bumped, if you do have the room you want, then you might enjoy the direction and pace that others are setting. The pace and help they give you in sighting and staying on course can make your race easier rather than harder. In cycling or running, when we are in a pack of people and the pack helps us finish our race faster than planned, we are usually more satisfied having been with others than if we had to ride or run the race alone.

Again, predictable behaviors of swimmers are that more competent swimmers stay on course and swim at a steadier pace. If you are swimming with another competent swimmer, you can share the work and responsibility for staying on course. When they see where they are going, that helps you too. When you confirm with your own look ahead that you are on course, then you are doubly assured. I actually like others doing the breaststroke while swimming with or past them in the open water. Although people swimming breaststroke take up more space in the water, they tend to point their bodies straight at the next buoy and are good guides. If you are parallel to them or right behind them, you can swim with or past them reliably.

A tempting situation that you might find yourself, while swimming with swimmers of the same level or slightly faster, is that it feels easy behind them so you want to pass them. Yet, once you are not behind them, the swimming is more difficult. Like cycling and running, you do get the aerodynamic or fluid benefit of drafting behind others that could give you the false impression that if you could only get to the front or off to the side, you could swim faster. While cycling, you soon find out that getting to the front of pack means that you are probably going at close to the same speed with much more effort. When fatigue develops, you want to be back in the pack following someone else while you recoup when you are cycling. In cycling, running and swimming, you want to be positioned at the front of the pack of athletes while not being the very front athlete guiding everyone else, unless your race plan is to pull others to the finish line.

So how do you get positioned towards the front of your pack. You get there with training that has you fitter than the other swimmers around you. If you can see better, breathe better and swim better than the next swimmer, you have the ability to go and stay where you want to be. If you are not fit, you will gradually, if not rapidly slide to the back of the pack of swimmers and then go off the back to swim alone or until someone else catches you.

The breaststroke can also help you keep your position in the pack of swimmers, too. While other swimmers behind you, may not like the idea of you doing the breaststroke in front of them, it helps you get them off of your feet and helps prevent them from swimming over the top of you. If a swimmer, like myself, is grabbing my feet or crowding me, then a few breaststroke kicks has them backing off and giving me the space that I want. The same happens in cycling or running where it's not uncommon to use your hand, arms or elbows to create more space around you in the pack. It's also the practice in cycling and running to look ahead and see if you are where you want to be in the pack. I know that there are some people that I would prefer following (bigger people swimming, riding or running at a steady pace) rather than smaller, squirrel like swimmers, riders and runners.

A worthy goal is to be fit enough to use other swimmers to help you race better. Whether you are in the first pack of swimmers or one of the latter packs of swimmers, work with others to help everyone swim faster and get out of the water safe and sound.

Race as a team. In cycling and running, it is more common to race as a team. In the Tour de France, everyone races for their team by taking turns and playing their roles on the team. In the Olympics though, where countries are allowed only one, two or three members, team work is less likely because individuals feel that this is their one shot at success. Somewhere in between swimming for your team and swimming for only yourself, might make the most sense. And sometimes, Plan A doesn't work for your team, yet Plan B still has someone on your team placing well rather than no one on the team doing well. Countries and certain individuals in the Olympics would have more medals if teammates worked together, like they do in the Tour de France. It's obvious that some athletes are stronger and others are faster. Usually races end with the strong swimmer winning or a faster swimmer following the strong swimmer sprinting past the stronger swimmer at the end to win.

You can even go beyond making plans with teammates by making plans on what other individuals or teams are likely to do. Some individuals or teams plan on the leading the race from start to finish. If you know that is likely, let them lead and follow them to the finish where you and your teammates' plan would be to pass them at the end. If you are really fit, you can also influence your competition by leading fast and then dropping behind them while they continue to swim, ride or run at too fast a pace. When they tire later, you will be able to pass them easily.

In a triathlon, though, where you have two more events to go, it is generally not worth sprinting to pass someone in the water who will then catch you on the bike or run. Pass your competition when you know they won't be able to pass you again if placing in front of others is important to you.

Swimming with others when we were young, was a "cat and mouse" game. As we improved, we found it easier to catch and tag others while swimming. Racing could also be a "cat and mouse" game. Practice and train to be the cat, rather than the mouse, if you want to swim and race better.

Chapter Seventeen – Feel for the water

Physically

It is important to have and maintain a feel for the water. Like an ice skater who skates daily versus the ice skater who puts their skates on once a year, it's important to swim frequently enough to improve your feel for the water. Swimming daily is a good start. If you can not swim daily, can you swim often enough to feel that you have not lost skill or feel since your last training session. People at the highest skill level in any profession say that they notice a downturn if they miss one day; and if they miss two days, then their fans start to notice. Even ten minutes of swimming helps you keep your feel for the water.

Physically it is important to swim regularly in order to see, breathe, position your weight, kick forward, and throw before you row. Because these actions are different then what we normally experience or do on land, we need to keep current with the water. Just working your exhale and knowing what you will be seeing is a worthwhile accomplishment if that is all the time you have. If you can think of positioning your weight and properly kicking on your back with your core engaged against gravity all the better. Practicing your roll up for air, so that the roll remains familiar, easy and predictable is important. Finally, using your arms to set the tone for your body, with throw before you row synchronization, makes every swim worthwhile no matter how much time you have.

Intellectually

It is not surprising that some of the best students are athletes. I would rather have someone come to class after a swim because they are awake and have been thinking for awhile. Calling someone a "dumb jock" is harsh, unkind and generally, not true. From my experience, athletes who want to learn their sport well take an interest in other subjects, as they then apply that knowledge to their favorite activity, their sport.

Swimming can be a particularly challenging intellectual activity, if you tend to be a thinker. It really helps to understand physics and some chemistry. Basic math skills are a given. It definitely helps to have a good head on your shoulders. My best swimmers have tended to be my brightest swimmers who not only adopted my techniques, they also adapted the techniques to themselves.

Paying attention and focusing on what you are doing in the moment, improves your concentration and intellectual capabilities. In changing swim conditions, choosing what you are going to think of, in order to swim better, makes you smarter. Not only can you become more intelligent, you can become more logical by trying hypotheses and coming to better conclusions, if you want to be a smart swimmer.

Emotionally

For me, swimming is the most refreshing, cleansing and relaxing sport that I have experienced. A swim always refreshes me, regardless of the time of day. A swim and a shower leaves me feeling cleaner than any other two activities that I can consider. I don't even mind the chlorine, killing the viruses and bacteria that have been hanging around me. Swimming slower than normal is relaxing, resting, like gliding and floating in space. Swimming is the most emotionally satisfying experience that I know.

Culture teaches that water renews us. In religion, water is used for baptism and blessing. In science, water is the "universal solvent", the safest solvent known to us. Water also helps to de-ionize and de-radiate us. Water calms us and flowing water, like the speed that many of us do swim, even more so.

Parents find that swimming is good for their children and for themselves. Having a swimming pool available, is a big plus for families. That water helps to "cool us off" is commonly understood.

Spiritually

For some people, it's not important that swimming becomes a spiritual exercise, yet it can be. Swimming is one of the quieter sports that allows for reflection. You feel lighter due to the buoyancy of the water and you could begin to notice more physical, intellectual, emotional and spiritual subtleties. Water is also thicker than air so your experience might transcend what you would normally expect.

Chapter Eighteen - Swimming Terminology

Every profession has it's jargon that tends to keep out others. Swimming is no different. If I could re-write a few swimming terms, here are some that I would make.

When you hear someone say, "Do four laps.", you might swim back and forth four times. In absolute swimming terms, a lap equals a length. Does that sound ridiculous? What word(s) do they use when they want someone to swim down and back, if a lap is not down and back? Most people will swim down and back or back and forth if you ask for a lap. Let's change the terminology so that a pool length is simply called a length. Two pool lengths, back and forth or down and back, would be called a lap.

How do you "Work on your catch."? What are you catching, water? Catching water is pretty hard. And after you catch and pull the water, do you let go? This is maybe like fishing where you catch and release and have nothing to show for it. In nautical terms isn't the arm really rowing when it is in the water? I call the underwater portion of the swim stroke simply the row and not the catch and pull.

The pull. I would say it is more like a row.

I would add the term throw for the action that the arm makes while out of the water moving forward. Many people would have a better swim stroke when they throw their arm into the water. Some people stroke the throw like they are stroking a cat though, which is bad technique. They are stroking in a tentative way like something might go wrong as they slowly reach in front of their heads. By calling that part of the stroke, the throw, people might swim with a better throwing action and better athleticism.

The kick can be called the kick as your feet are kicking. However, the counting of how many times a person kicks could be changed. The two beat kick becomes simply the one beat kick or one kick as each foot is only kicking once and not twice. The four beat kick could be called two kicks as each foot is moving twice and not for times per arm. The six beat kick becomes three kicks as each foot is kicking three times while you take two strokes, one with left arm and one with your left arm. Beginners don't even count their kicks. I have seen twelve beat kicks, so is there a point where we say no more, this is getting to hard to count? One kick per arm stroke is just one kick, like walking.

The flotation device that goes between your legs is called a pull buoy. Again, are we pulling a flotation device which is not supposed to move between the legs? Why is "the pull" a rowing action when swimming and the "pull buoy" a flotation device that you keep stationery between your legs while you swim. You could rename the flotation device held between your legs and send it to me.

I do like the terms swim paddles for the paddles that you put on your hands that can help your hands row under water.

Technical terminology can change. If you think of other swimming terms that are confusing to anti-swimmers and don't help to promote the understanding of the sport, please send them to me for a good laugh too.

Your fin begins with your finge...

Thumbswimmers...

Chapter Nineteen – Body Maintenance

Showering before swimming is a very good idea. While the shower might feel cold, if you and others don't shower before you swim, you are polluting the water. The most notable offenders are perfumes, deodorants and colognes. The products that people use to smell "better" pollute the water and stink when combined with water. Unfortunately, you can even taste someone's deodorant, etc., which is like tasting their arm pits. Natural body oils also pollute the water. Anything that could have been showered off your body stays in the pool after you leave the pool. Polluting the pool water with deodorants, colognes, perfumes and body oils increases the demand that more chemicals be added to the pool water to handle what could have been rinsed off. If you think you could be wearing anything that you don't want to drink, please shower.

Foggy goggles are often the result of the temperature of the water being different than the temperature of the goggles. Like a foggy windshield in a car, there are actions that you can take for foggy goggles. The simplest action is to throw your goggles into the water before you swim. Before long, the goggles will be at the same temperature as the water and the goggles won't fog up. You can also wipe them with your thumbs up after you swim awhile if they fog up because the goggles did not acclimate the first time. Some swimmers use spit, toothpaste and anti-fog products so their goggles don't fog in the first place. As I have grown more patient in letting the goggles stay in the water before I put them on to swim, I seldom have had to do anything more than wipe them off after a hundred yards and then the goggles are fine for the rest of the swim. Again, the more we can do to keep toothpaste and anti-fog products out of the water, the better.

If you get water in your ears, most people can pinch and tug downward the lowest part of their ear to drain the water. Try that the next time you have water in your ear as it is better for your neck than throwing your head to one side and then the other over and over. Pinching and pulling own the sides of your ear by the level of your ear lobe will often drain the water out of your ear without any drama or trauma.

Vinegar and alcohol is a great combination for your ears. Using a solution of two parts vinegar and one part alcohol effectively rinses your ears and restores your ears pH level. You can make this solution at home and save yourself quite a bit of money as vinegar and rubbing alcohol are inexpensive products. When I feel an earache coming or have an earache, I use vinegar and alcohol to massage the sore ear while the solution is in the ear. Sometimes it takes a couple rinses and massage to remove the soreness of the earache. Since, I have started this routine, I have not had any earaches requiring a trip to the doctor. Preventive maintenance of your ears is easy, inexpensive and pays off. Rinse your ears every other day as a good health habit.

Chlorine is good in the water but not on your swim suit and you. Chlorine is a wonder product. It kills viruses and bacteria effectively. If water is the universal solvent, chlorine is the universal germ killer. If you can smell or taste chlorine in the water, either too much chlorine was added or the other chemicals that they use to balance or offset the chlorine are not correct. While you can swim in a pool where you can detect the chlorine, it's up to you how much your body can take. Showering and soaping down your skin and your swim suit after swimming in a pool is a good habit. The sooner and more thoroughly you can get the chlorine off, the better. So while I like the idea of a chlorine swim to kill any of the germs or viruses on me and others that we are not aware of while we swim, I don't need a coating of chlorine on my skin for the remainder of the day that would dry my skin out.

Salt water is a healthy alternative to chlorine. If your pool uses salt rather than chlorine all the better. Do rinse off before you get in the pool and afterward and continue to take care of your ears.

Rinsing your sinus cavities with salt water after a swim is a good practice to prevent sinus infections. While it is not an easy habit to adopt, I have had fewer problems since rinsing every other day with a NeilMed® Sinus Rinse solution of salt water. The bottle allows you to rinse out your sinuses completely. My doctor recommended it to me during a serious sinus infection. It worked and I have been using it since that time to prevent sinus infections.

Shaving down used to be only for competitive swimmers. Now, shaving your body has gained an aesthetic acceptance even outside of swimming. People pay good money for laser and other hair removal treatments. Less hair now seems to be more socially acceptable; so, if you want to shave down for swimming, you probably won't be shunned by anyone. Competitive cyclists have also been shaving down for years because it easier to treat road rash and skin injuries when there is no hair in the way. Triathletes shave down because shaving helps them to be faster in the water, stay cleaner and dry faster. One of the big differences that I did notice is how fast the body dries after a swim without the wet hair retaining water, which is an advantage for someone who tends to feel cold after a swim. Shaving is an activity that takes practice and frequency if you are going to do it or it will feel like you are shaving for the first time over and over. Some men can shave their face and body in twenty minutes or less because they are used to the routine and do it two or three times a week. While shaving is not a requirement for swimming or competing in triathlons, it might become a personal preference even for the casual swimmer and triathlete.

Hair care is another personal matter. Chlorine tends to bleach the hair and make it feel coarse or thick. Showering your hair before you swim and wearing a swim cap reduces the amount of chlorine that ends up in your hair. Washing the chlorine out when you are done swimming, with a product that works for your hair is the second way to protect your hair. Using common baking soda in the wash and rinse process also offsets the chlorine. Olive oil in your hair helps if you don't mind the olive oil. These are some of my suggestions to try over time so that chlorine in your hair becomes less of an issue for you.

Nail care is very easy after a swim. The nails are clean and soft for filing or clipping.

Eye care is usually covered with a good pair of goggles. Good goggles do not leak and that was the number one problem with eye care. The quality and variety of goggles and masks is now at such a high level, that there is no need to be satisfied with poor fitting eye wear in the pool. Some brands also can fit precision lenses for those who need glasses even while swimming or siting. Before you spend money on prescription goggles, try the natural refraction that the water offers to correct your vision and you might be surprised to find that the water refraction takes care of your vision.

Suction marks from goggles or masks still seem to be a problem, especially as we get older, even though there has been a huge improvement in the cushioning and water seal of many goggles. The shape of your face and eyes determine the goggle or mask that works for you and if you can find a goggle that leaves less of an imprint on your skin for a shorter amount of time, buy it. There are also goggles that fit very close to the eye sockets that are popular with young swimmers. If you want to try something that might eliminate suction marks on your skin, the socket goggles tend to cost even less than masks or heavily padded goggles.

Skin care begins with a shower before you get in the water. It continues with the soap down and shower after you skin. Skin care could include shaving. And, it could include olive oil. Extra virgin olive oil is a relatively inexpensive natural skin product. People have been using olive oil and other natural oils for thousands of years. Try using a natural oil that is inexpensive and reduces the risk of chemical compounding.

Swim suits vary a great deal, too. Some suits hold up much better in chlorine than others do. I have had suits last as little as a month and others last for years. FINIS® had or has a material that has lasted me three years and the seams are coming apart rather than the material thinning or sagging from the chlorine. You will probably have to shop until you find the right suit for you and then hope they don't discontinue the suit. Suit styles also change. The short, bikini brief suit was popular for men and women during and after WWII because of the shortage in materials that the war brought. I guess you could also say that the briefer the swim suit the greener, more environmentally friendly it is these days. However, more often than not swimmers and triathletes are conscious of their appearance and prefer "jammers" to cover everything from their waist to almost their knees. Suits can also reduce drag in the water if you pay more money for a swim suit that is slicker and tighter than your skin.

Chapter Twenty – Measurement

Most people want to measure their progress swimming. Nearly everyone wants to know if they are doing better and better is usually associated with the time it takes to swim a distance. For many triathletes, doing better is swimming faster or as fast with less effort. Triathletes are sometimes satisfied with their time; yet, they are not satisfied with the effort it took, because the effort leaves them unable to ride or run as fast after their swim.

An important measurement is knowing on which breathing side do you swim faster. One side tends to be faster than the other side due to better skill level, weight positioning, flexibility, etc.. Time your swim when breathing solely to your left and then time your right side. Work to become faster on both sides. Interestingly, some swimmers make more rapid gains on the side that they have been neglecting. Due to less muscle memory on the side that they used less, they might make progress faster on the weak side that they used to ignore.

Measure your two stroke swimming times on one side and then the other for one hundred yards. The two measurements probably produced differing times and feelings. It is important to know your faster side because perception can deceive you. If you are swimming correctly, you have both arms working together with a throw/row regardless of the side you are breathing to while swimming. Once both arms are working together, does a right hand throw and a left hand row really work better than your left hand throw and right hand row? The dominance that being right handed or left handed creates is somewhat negated by using both hands together with my swimming technique where the work is divided with a combined throw/row action versus row, row, row. And in the open water, where there are no lane lines to guide you, your "slower" side might be the side that has you swimming straighter so you don't go off course. Swimming straighter adds speed, too.

A two stroke freestyle pace as fast as your three stroke freestyle pace (or vice versa) is another measurement worth tracking. Most people are faster at one or the other because of their proficiencies and deficiencies. When you race, go with your strengths. When you train though, narrow the difference between your strengths and weaknesses. Two and three stroke swimming places different demands on you and it is valuable to be able to swim either way or you are limiting yourself.

Strokes plus seconds of time optimization is a good individual measurement. It is not a good comparison measurement between yourself and other swimmers, though. I would not compare the total strokes plus seconds of a two hundred pound swimmer versus total strokes plus seconds of a hundred pound swimmer. They are two different players. Like a center and guard in basketball, they are both going to score their points; yet, they will score in different ways. The guard is going to dribble and shoot more jump shots while the center is going to dribble less and dunk more in a game of one on one.

Some call strokes plus seconds for fifty yards a "golf" score because the total of strokes plus seconds approximates the game of golf. For example, thirty strokes and fifty-one seconds is a score of eighty-one. The measurement is designed to measure efficiency by a combination of stroke or time reduction. This is a measurement that favors bigger swimmers as bigger swimmers start out with the physical advantage of taking fewer strokes. It is an unfair comparison between say a small woman and a large man who swim the exact same time, yet the small woman took more strokes. I would not conclude the smaller woman was not as efficient as the larger man because her "golf" score was higher because of her taking more strokes. I have seen on some blogs where swimmers are touting their "golf" scores in comparison to others and this is not good. It is good to improve on your golf score; yet don't compare your score to others. Even the difference in skin surface, wrinkled versus smooth, effects the scores. Swimmers do benefit if they lower their own scores, especially when it is real seconds that are coming off the score. Taking strokes off is secondary though, because one could take strokes off of their score by kicking more. Imagine a stroke count as low as one or two stokes for a length because the swimmer kicked the entire way. Some swimmers have such good kicks that they could achieve a low "golf" score by just kicking and adding their seconds. One stroke plus sixty seconds is a score of sixty-one, if you want to get ridiculous with "golf" scores.

Minimizing your time differences between freestyle and other swim strokes is a worthwhile measurement. It definitely pays to have other stroke options and physical skills. Measure the time it takes to swim fifty or a hundred yards in freestyle, backstroke and breaststroke. You want to measure and improve your slower strokes so the difference in time or speed lessens. While you probably won't be swimming backstroke or breaststroke for long stretches in a triathlon or open water swim, it could be a problem if you can't. Few people lack the skill, strength and total control of the situation to swim the entire distance without taking a backstroke or breaststroke. I think if more swimmers did planned breaks with backstroke or breaststroke, they would go even faster and stay on course better, too.

Measure your twenty-five yard speed, before your swim becomes anaerobic. While I am not a big fan of anaerobic swimming for older athletes, you can still swim fast for twenty-five yards to measure your speed. Measure your twenty-five yard freestyle, backstroke and breaststroke to know your top speed. Try to improve on that time through better technique. Yet, it may be the case that God made you only so fast physiologically. All people have physical speed limitations and even the fastest person reaches a point where they can't make themselves faster, legally.

Besides knowing how fast you are at twenty-five yards, it's helpful to know how well you maintain that speed over a longer distance. The slower swimmer could work and become better at five hundred or five thousand yards than the swimmer who is faster at fifty yards. Sometimes we do have sprinters trying to see how many distances they can dominate. One person might want to own all the records from fifty yards to five hundred yards. Usually though, the competition is so stiff in the sprints, that the top sprinters don't try to win at longer distances where they haven't had success. On the other hand, swimmers with less speed at fifty yards come to realize that they are never going to win or place regularly in the sprints. These swimmers start swimming longer and longer distances in training and racing hoping to gain endurance so they can win or place more regularly.

Measure your ten minute speed to begin to learn your aerobic condition and speed over distance. While twenty-five yards is neither predominantly aerobic or anaerobic, swimming for ten minutes straight is predominantly aerobic. You could go anaerobic during the ten minutes; yet, eighty percent or more of your final results are due to your technique and aerobic capacity. Ten minutes is a good measurement for triathletes because it approximates the time it takes to swim a sprint triathlon.

Measure your thirty minute speed during your time trials. Thirty minutes of swimming is over ninety percent aerobic. You may be able to hold your thirty minute pace for nearly an hour because it is aerobic. Over a period of thirty minutes, it does not pay to go anaerobic until the very end of the thirty minutes in order to pick up a few more seconds. If you go anaerobic earlier, the rest of your swim will be miserable trying to recover and hold your pace. Thirty minutes is a good measurement for triathletes as it approximates the time it takes to swim an international or Olympic distance triathlon.

Measure your hour speed every three months. Measure your hour distance even more often than that if you are swimming that long or longer in triathlons or open water swim competitions. An hour swim is aerobic ninety-eight percent of the time that you are swimming. It could be one hundred percent aerobic. You might find yourself not much slower, keeping the swim purely aerobic, rather than going into oxygen debt to squeeze out a few more seconds at the end.

Regardless of time, consider that better results could be just feeling better, too. If you measure your health, in that you feel better after a swim, that is a worthwhile measurement, too. Lowering your heart rate and getting back to healthy blood levels for cholesterol, etc. are also worthwhile measurements. Think of other ways to measure the quality of your swim rather than just the time it takes to swim a given distance.

Can Exercise Keep You Young?

By *GRETCHEN REYNOLDS*

We all know that physical activity is beneficial in countless ways, but even so, Dr. Mark Tarnopolsky, a professor of pediatrics at McMaster University in Hamilton, Ontario, was startled to discover that exercise kept a strain of mice from becoming gray prematurely.

But shiny fur was the least of its benefits. Indeed, in heartening new research published last week in The Proceedings of the National Academy of Sciences, exercise reduced or eliminated almost every detrimental effect of aging in mice that had been genetically programmed to grow old at an accelerated pace.

In the experiment, Dr. Tarnopolsky and his colleagues used lab rodents that carry a genetic mutation affecting how well their bodies repair malfunctioning mitochondria, which are tiny organelles within cells. Mitochondria combine oxygen and nutrients to create fuel for the cells — they are microscopic power generators.

Mitochrondria have their own DNA, distinct from the cell's own genetic material, and they multiply on their own. But in the process, mitochondria can accumulate small genetic mutations, which under normal circumstances are corrected by specialized repair systems within the cell. Over time, as we age, the number of mutations begins to outstrip the system's ability to make repairs, and mitochondria start malfunctioning and dying.

Many scientists consider the loss of healthy mitochondria to be an important underlying cause of aging in mammals. As resident mitochondria falter, the cells they fuel wither or die. Muscles shrink, brain volume drops, hair falls out or loses its pigmentation, and soon enough we are, in appearance and beneath the surface, old.

The mice that Dr. Tarnopolsky and his colleagues used lacked the primary mitochondrial repair mechanism, so they developed

172

malfunctioning mitochondria early in their lives, as early as 3 months of age, the human equivalent of age 20. By the time they reached 8 months, or their early 60s in human terms, the animals were extremely frail and decrepit, with spindly muscles, shrunken brains, enlarged hearts, shriveled gonads and patchy, graying fur. Listless, they barely moved around their cages. All were dead before reaching a year of age.

Except the mice that exercised.

Half of the mice were allowed to run on a wheel for 45 minutes three times a week, beginning at 3 months. These rodent runners were required to maintain a fairly brisk pace, Dr. Tarnopolsky said: "It was about like a person running a 50- or 55-minute 10K." (A 10K race is 6.2 miles.) The mice continued this regimen for five months.

At 8 months, when their sedentary lab mates were bald, frail and dying, the running rats remained youthful. They had full pelts of dark fur, no salt-and-pepper shadings. They also had maintained almost all of their muscle mass and brain volume. Their gonads were normal, as were their hearts. They could balance on narrow rods, the showoffs.

But perhaps most remarkable, although they still harbored the mutation that should have affected mitochondrial repair, they had more mitochondria over all and far fewer with mutations than the sedentary mice had. At 1 year, none of the exercising mice had died of natural causes. (Some were sacrificed to compare their cellular health to that of the unexercised mice, all of whom were, by that age, dead.)

The researchers were surprised by the magnitude of the impact that exercise had on the animals' aging process, Dr. Tarnopolsky said. He and his colleagues had expected to find that exercise would affect mitochondrial health in muscles, including the heart, since past research had shown a connection. They had not expected that it would affect every tissue and bodily system studied.

Other studies, including a number from Dr. Tarnopolsky's own lab, have also found that exercise affects the course of aging, but none has shown such a comprehensive effect. And precisely how exercise alters the aging process remains unknown. In this experiment, running resulted in an upsurge in the rodents' production of a protein known as PGC-1alpha, which regulates genes involved in metabolism and energy creation, including mitochondrial function. Exercise also sparked the repair of malfunctioning mitochondria through a mechanism outside the known repair pathway; in these mutant mice, that pathway didn't exist, but their mitochondria were nonetheless being repaired.

Dr. Tarnopolsky is currently overseeing a number of experiments that he expects will help to elucidate the specific physiological mechanisms. But for now, he said, the lesson of his experiment and dozens like it is unambiguous. "Exercise alters the course of aging," he said.

Although in this experiment, the activity was aerobic and strenuous, Dr. Tarnopolsky is not convinced that either is absolutely necessary for benefits. Studies of older humans have shown that weightlifting can improve mitochondrial health, he said, as can moderate endurance exercise. Although there is probably a threshold amount of exercise that is necessary to affect physiological aging, Dr. Tarnopolsky said, "anything is better than nothing." If you haven't been active in the past, he continued, start walking five minutes a day, then begin to increase your activity level.

The potential benefits have attractions even for the young. While Dr. Tarnopolsky, a lifelong athlete, noted with satisfaction that active, aged mice kept their hair, his younger graduate students were far more interested in the animals' robust gonads. Their testicles and ovaries hadn't shrunk, unlike those of sedentary elderly mice.

Dr. Tarnopolsky's students were impressed. "I think they all exercise now," he said.

CPSIA information can be obtained at www.ICGtesting.com
Printed in the USA
LVOW012058150213

320346LV00018B/996/P